TORONTO

TRAVEL GUIDE
2024

---

*A COMPREHENSIVE GUIDE TO THE
CITY OF TORONTO*

CARLTON B. MAYNARD

2024 EDITION

CN Tower
Tower in Toronto, Canada

TABLE OF CONTENTS

Cavalcade of Lights,Nathan Phillips Square

WELCOME TO TORONTO

1

INTRODUCTION

Welcome to Toronto, a city where the heartbeat of diversity harmonizes with the rhythm of modernity. As you embark on this journey through our Toronto Travel Guide, prepare to be enchanted by a metropolis that effortlessly blends cultural richness, urban vibrancy, and natural splendor. In 2024, Toronto stands as a tapestry of experiences waiting to be unfolded, each thread representing the unique charm of its neighborhoods, the breathtaking allure of its attractions, and the warmth of its people.

Whether you're a first-time visitor or a returning explorer, Toronto unveils a myriad of wonders that cater to every taste and curiosity. From the iconic silhouette of the CN Tower piercing the skyline to the quaint cobblestone streets of the Distillery District, our guide is your key to unlocking the city's secrets and discovering the hidden gems that make Toronto a captivating destination.

Join us as we navigate through the diverse tapestry of neighborhoods, delve into the cultural tapestry of museums and theaters, and savor the flavors of a culinary scene that reflects the city's global influences. Feel the pulsating energy of the nightlife, find tranquility in lush parks, and embark on day trips that promise unforgettable adventures.

Toronto isn't just a place; it's an immersive experience waiting to captivate your senses and create lasting memories. So, let this guide be your companion as you explore the heart and soul of Toronto, a city that beats with a rhythm uniquely its own. Your journey begins here, promising a symphony of experiences that will resonate in your heart long after you've bid farewell to the mesmerizing landscapes of Toronto.

Overview of Toronto

Toronto, a city that pulsates with life and beckons to the soul, stands as a testament to the harmonious blend of diversity, innovation, and boundless charm.

As you step into the embrace of Canada's largest metropolis, you'll find yourself immersed in a world where modern skyscrapers gracefully coexist with historic architecture, and where the echoes of countless cultures create a symphony of experiences.

Nestled along the shores of Lake Ontario, Toronto invites you to explore its diverse neighborhoods, each a tapestry of unique stories and vibrant characters. From the glittering lights of downtown to the eclectic artistry of Kensington Market, the city unfolds before you like a captivating novel, each chapter revealing a new facet of its rich identity.

Toronto's skyline is crowned by the iconic CN Tower, a soaring testament to the city's aspirations and a beacon that guides you through a landscape dotted with green spaces, cultural landmarks, and a thriving culinary scene. Museums and galleries showcase the city's commitment to the arts, while the warmth of its residents reflects the true heart of Toronto.

But Toronto is more than just a collection of landmarks; it's a living, breathing entity that invites you to immerse yourself in its rhythm. Whether you're strolling through lush parks, savoring international cuisines, or delving into the diverse cultural experiences, Toronto promises a journey that transcends the ordinary.

Join us as we unravel the secrets of this enchanting city, guiding you through the avenues of exploration, the festivals that pulse with energy, and the hidden corners that hold the city's most treasured stories. Toronto is more than a destination; it's an emotion waiting to be felt, a melody waiting to be heard. Let this guide be your passport to the heart of Toronto, where every moment is a page-turner in the story of your unforgettable adventure.

What's New in 2024

In 2024, Toronto is poised to unveil a tapestry of new experiences and attractions, adding fresh colors to the vibrant canvas of this dynamic city. As you explore the metropolis, anticipate exciting developments and novel opportunities that promise to redefine your Toronto experience:

1. Innovative Skyline Additions:

Witness the ever-changing skyline with the addition of innovative architectural marvels, each contributing to Toronto's reputation as a city at the forefront of modern design. New skyscrapers and iconic structures are set to reshape the horizon.

2. Cultural District Expansions:

Toronto's commitment to the arts expands further, with the growth of existing cultural districts and the emergence of new ones. Expect additional galleries, theaters, and immersive art installations that showcase the city's thriving creative spirit.

3. Revitalized Waterfront Spaces:

The lakefront undergoes a transformation, offering revitalized public spaces, scenic promenades, and enhanced recreational areas. Enjoy stunning views of Lake Ontario while indulging in waterfront activities that seamlessly blend urban and natural elements.

4. Innovative Technological Experiences:

Toronto, a hub of technological innovation, introduces cutting-edge experiences that leverage the latest advancements. Look forward to interactive exhibits, augmented reality installations, and tech-driven attractions that redefine the boundaries of entertainment.

5. Sustainable Initiatives:

Embracing its commitment to sustainability, Toronto unveils new eco-friendly initiatives and green spaces. From urban gardens to sustainable architecture, the city continues to prioritize environmental consciousness, providing visitors with a green and responsible travel experience.

6. Culinary Scene Evolution:

Toronto's diverse culinary scene evolves with the introduction of unique dining concepts, fusion cuisines, and innovative gastronomic experiences. Explore neighborhoods where food is not just a meal but a journey through global flavors.

7. Community Events and Festivals:

Toronto's calendar is enriched with new community events and festivals that celebrate the city's multicultural identity. Immerse yourself in the festivities, from street parties to cultural celebrations, fostering a sense of unity and inclusivity.

8. Enhanced Transportation Options:

Efforts to improve accessibility and connectivity result in enhanced transportation options. Experience the convenience of updated public transit, bike-sharing initiatives, and pedestrian-friendly developments that make navigating the city even more enjoyable.

As you embark on your Toronto adventure in 2024, anticipate a city in perpetual motion, embracing change while preserving its rich heritage. This guide is your key to unlocking the door to these new experiences, ensuring you don't miss a beat in this ever-evolving urban landscape.

GETTING TO TORONTO

Getting to Toronto is an exciting start to your adventure in this dynamic city. With various transportation options available, reaching Toronto is convenient and accessible. Whether you're arriving by air, train, or bus, here's a brief overview to guide you:

Toronto Pearson International Airport (YYZ) is the primary airport serving the city, offering a comprehensive network of domestic and international flights. Upon arrival, you'll find various transportation options, including taxis, airport shuttles, and public transit, making it easy to reach your destination within the city.

Via Rail provides efficient train services connecting Toronto with major cities across Canada. Union Station, located in downtown Toronto, serves as a central hub for train travel, offering a convenient entry point to the heart of the city.

Long-distance buses, such as Greyhound and Megabus, connect Toronto with cities in Canada and the United States. The Toronto Coach Terminal, situated near downtown, serves as a major hub for intercity bus services, facilitating a smooth transition to the city center.

Once in Toronto, navigating the city is seamless with an extensive public transportation system. The Toronto Transit Commission (TTC) operates buses, streetcars, and subways, providing efficient and affordable transportation options. Taxis, ride-sharing services, biking, and walking are also popular ways to explore the vibrant neighborhoods of Toronto.

As you arrive in Toronto, the diverse and welcoming atmosphere of the city awaits, promising a rich tapestry of experiences to unfold during your stay.

Transportation Options

Toronto offers a diverse range of transportation options to facilitate easy and efficient travel throughout the city. Whether you're arriving from afar or navigating within Toronto itself, these transportation choices cater to various preferences and needs. From air travel to ground transportation, the city's well-connected network ensures a seamless and enjoyable journey for residents and visitors alike. Once in Toronto, explore the city's neighborhoods with public transit, taxis, ride-sharing services, or embrace the pedestrian-friendly atmosphere by walking or biking. The array of transportation choices reflects Toronto's commitment to accessibility and convenience, allowing you to traverse the city with ease and immerse yourself in the vibrant tapestry of experiences it has to offer.

Air Travel

Toronto, a global hub, welcomes travelers from around the world through its primary airport, Toronto Pearson International Airport (YYZ). Navigating air travel to Toronto is a seamless experience with a range of international and domestic flights connecting to this bustling metropolis.

* Toronto Pearson International Airport (YYZ):
   - As Canada's busiest airport, Pearson International offers a world-class travel experience. Located approximately 22.5 kilometers (14 miles) northwest of downtown Toronto, the airport serves as a major gateway to the city and beyond.

* International Flights:

- Toronto Pearson is well-connected to cities worldwide, facilitating international travel with airlines covering various continents. Expect a smooth and efficient immigration process upon arrival.

* Domestic Flights:

- For domestic travelers, Toronto Pearson is a central hub connecting major cities across Canada. Enjoy the convenience of direct flights and efficient connections within the country.

* Ground Transportation from the Airport:

- Numerous transportation options are available for the journey from the airport to downtown Toronto, including:
    - Taxis: Readily available outside the terminals.
    - Airport Shuttles: Scheduled services offering shared rides to popular destinations.
    - Public Transit: The UP Express train provides a quick and direct connection to Union Station in downtown Toronto.
    - Rental Cars: Multiple car rental agencies operate at the airport.

* Airport Amenities:

- Toronto Pearson boasts a range of amenities, including shopping outlets, dining options, lounges, and services to ensure a comfortable stay during layovers or before exploring the city.

Whether you're arriving for business or leisure, Toronto Pearson International Airport serves as the gateway to a city brimming with cultural richness, vibrant neighborhoods, and unparalleled experiences. As you disembark, get ready to embark on a journey through the heart of Toronto.

Train Services

Toronto is seamlessly connected by efficient train services, offering a scenic and comfortable way to reach the heart of the city. Via Rail, Canada's national rail service, provides excellent connectivity to Toronto from various cities across the country.

* Via Rail:

- Via Rail offers a comprehensive network of trains, connecting Toronto with major cities including Montreal, Ottawa, and Vancouver. The trains provide a comfortable and picturesque journey, allowing travelers to relax and enjoy the landscapes.

* Union Station:

- Union Station, located in downtown Toronto, serves as a central hub for Via Rail services. This historic transportation hub is not only an essential transit point but also an architectural gem, reflecting the city's rich history.

* High-Speed Rail (HFR):

- Via Rail's High Frequency Rail (HFR) service, a modern high-speed rail project, is set to enhance connectivity between Toronto and nearby cities. This initiative aims to provide faster and more frequent train services, further improving the efficiency of rail travel.

* Convenience and Comfort:

- Train travel to Toronto is known for its convenience and comfort. Passengers can enjoy amenities such as spacious seating, dining services, and scenic views along the journey.

* Connecting to the City:

- Upon arrival at Union Station, travelers have easy access to various transportation options, including taxis, ride-sharing services, and public transit. Union Station's central location makes it convenient for visitors to explore Toronto's downtown and beyond.

Whether you're arriving from nearby cities or embarking on a cross-country adventure, train services to Toronto offer a delightful introduction to the city. As you step off the train, you'll find yourself immersed in the vibrant energy of Toronto, ready to explore its diverse neighborhoods and cultural treasures.

Bus Services

Toronto's accessibility extends to a well-established network of long-distance bus services, connecting the city with destinations across Canada and the United States. Several reputable bus companies provide a convenient and affordable means of reaching Toronto.

* Greyhound:
- Greyhound, a prominent bus service, connects Toronto with numerous cities in both Canada and the United States. The Toronto Coach Terminal

serves as a major hub for Greyhound services, offering reliable and comfortable long-distance travel.

* Megabus:

\- Megabus provides a budget-friendly option for travelers heading to Toronto. With modern amenities and a focus on affordability, Megabus offers routes to and from various cities, enhancing the accessibility of Toronto as a travel destination.

* Toronto Coach Terminal:

\- The Toronto Coach Terminal, conveniently located near downtown Toronto, is a central hub for long-distance bus services. This transportation hub ensures easy access to the heart of the city upon arrival.

* Comfortable and Cost-Effective Travel:

\- Bus travel to Toronto is known for its cost-effectiveness and convenience. Passengers can enjoy comfortable seating, rest stops, and the option to choose from various schedules to suit their travel preferences.

* Connecting with Toronto's Transit System:

- Upon arriving at the Toronto Coach Terminal, travelers have access to various transportation options, including taxis, ride-sharing services, and Toronto's extensive public transit system. This facilitates seamless exploration of the city and its diverse neighborhoods.

Whether you're arriving from a nearby city or planning a cross-border journey, bus services to Toronto provide a practical and efficient travel option. As you step off the bus, you'll find yourself at the doorstep of a city ready to unfold its cultural richness and urban vibrancy.

Getting Around the City

Once you've arrived in Toronto, navigating the city is a seamless and enjoyable experience with a variety of transportation options at your disposal. Whether you prefer the efficiency of public transit, the convenience of taxis, or the freedom of exploring on foot, Toronto offers a diverse range of choices for getting around.

* **Public Transportation (TTC):**

- The Toronto Transit Commission (TTC) operates an extensive network of buses, streetcars, and subways, providing efficient and affordable transportation throughout the city. Consider purchasing a Presto card for easy access to all public transit options.

* Subway:

- Toronto's subway system is a quick and efficient way to traverse the city, especially during peak hours. With four major lines covering key areas, the subway offers a rapid means of transportation.

* Buses and Streetcars:

- The TTC's bus and streetcar routes cover neighborhoods and areas not directly served by the subway. These options provide a comprehensive way to explore different parts of the city.

* Taxis and Ride-Sharing:

- Taxis are readily available throughout Toronto, offering a convenient and comfortable mode of transportation. Additionally, ride-sharing services like Uber and Lyft provide an alternative for door-to-door travel.

* Biking:

- Toronto is a bike-friendly city with dedicated bike lanes and trails. Renting a bike is a popular and eco-friendly way to explore the city at your own pace. Several bike-sharing programs are available for short rides.

* Walking:

- Many of Toronto's neighborhoods are pedestrian-friendly, with attractions, shops, and restaurants within walking distance. Stroll through iconic areas like Yonge-Dundas Square or explore the picturesque streets of the Distillery District on foot.

* Car Rentals:

- If you prefer the flexibility of driving, various car rental agencies operate in the city. Keep in mind that traffic conditions can vary, and parking may be limited in certain areas.

Navigating Toronto is not just a means of transportation; it's an opportunity to immerse yourself in the city's vibrant neighborhoods, cultural attractions, and diverse landscapes. Choose the mode of transportation that suits your preferences, and get ready to explore the dynamic and welcoming metropolis of Toronto.

Public Transportation

Toronto's public transportation system, operated by the Toronto Transit Commission (TTC), is a reliable and extensive network that efficiently connects the city's neighborhoods and attractions. Whether you're traveling by bus, streetcar, or subway, the TTC provides a convenient way to explore Toronto. Here's a closer look at the key aspects of public transportation in the city:

* **Subway**:
  - Toronto's subway system is one of the fastest ways to navigate the city. It consists of four major lines: Line 1 (Yonge-University), Line 2 (Bloor-Danforth), Line 3 (Scarborough), and Line 4 (Sheppard). The subway operates from early morning until late at night, making it a popular choice for commuters and visitors alike.

* **Buses and Streetcars**:
  - The extensive bus and streetcar network covers neighborhoods and areas not served by the subway.

Buses operate on a wide range of routes, providing flexibility for reaching different parts of the city. Streetcars, especially prevalent in downtown Toronto, offer a unique and scenic way to travel.

* Presto Card:

- To streamline your public transit experience, consider using a Presto card. This contactless smart card allows for easy and convenient access to all TTC services, including subways, buses, and streetcars. The card can be loaded with funds and used for seamless transfers between different modes of transportation.

* Fares and Passes:

- TTC fares are based on a distance-based system, with additional costs for connecting routes. Various fare options are available, including single rides, day passes, and monthly passes. Visitors can choose the option that best suits their travel needs.

* Schedules and Routes:

- The TTC provides detailed schedules and route maps for buses, streetcars, and subways. These resources make it easy for both residents and visitors to plan their journeys and explore the city efficiently.

* Accessibility:

- The TTC is committed to providing accessible transportation for all. Many subway stations and vehicles are equipped with features to assist individuals with disabilities, ensuring that public transit is inclusive and accommodating.

Toronto's public transportation system is not just a means of getting from point A to point B; it's an integral part of the city's character and culture. Whether you're commuting to work, exploring iconic attractions, or discovering hidden gems, the TTC is your ticket to a seamless and enriching Toronto experience.

Taxis and Ride-Sharing

Navigating Toronto's diverse neighborhoods or reaching specific destinations with ease is made convenient through the availability of taxis and ride-sharing services. These transportation options offer flexibility and door-to-door service, ensuring a comfortable and efficient travel experience.

* Taxis:

- Traditional taxis are a common sight in Toronto, providing on-demand service throughout the city. You can easily find taxis at designated taxi stands, outside major transportation hubs, or by flagging one down on the street. Taxis offer a reliable and straightforward mode of transportation, with fares based on a meter.

* Ride-Sharing Services:

- Popular ride-sharing services such as Uber and Lyft operate in Toronto, offering a convenient alternative to traditional taxis. These services can be accessed through mobile apps, allowing you to request rides, track your driver, and make cashless transactions. Ride-sharing provides additional flexibility, especially during peak travel times.

* Accessibility:

- Taxis and ride-sharing services in Toronto are committed to providing accessible transportation. Many vehicles are equipped to accommodate passengers with mobility challenges, and ride-sharing apps often allow users to request accessible vehicles when needed.

* Airport Transportation:
   - Taxis and ride-sharing services are readily available at Toronto Pearson International Airport (YYZ) for convenient airport transportation. Pick-up points are well-marked, making it easy for travelers to access these services upon arrival.

* Costs and Payments:
   - Taxis typically operate on metered fares, while ride-sharing services provide fare estimates upfront. Payment for both taxis and ride-sharing can be made using cash or through the respective app's digital payment system. Be sure to confirm the payment method with your driver.

* Service Availability:
   - Taxis and ride-sharing services are available throughout the city, making them suitable for both short trips within neighborhoods and longer journeys between different parts of Toronto.

Whether you choose a traditional taxi or opt for the convenience of ride-sharing, these transportation options offer a door-to-door solution for exploring Toronto at your own pace. With easy accessibility, reliable service, and the added convenience of digital payments, taxis and ride-sharing contribute to the diverse and accessible transportation landscape of the city.

Biking and Walking

Exploring Toronto on foot or by bike provides a unique and intimate way to experience the city's diverse neighborhoods, scenic landscapes, and vibrant streets. With dedicated paths, picturesque trails, and pedestrian-friendly areas, Toronto invites residents and visitors alike to embrace active modes of transportation.

* BIKING

- Bike Rentals: Numerous bike rental services operate in Toronto, offering an accessible and eco-friendly means of transportation. Pick up a bike from rental stations scattered throughout the city, and embark on a journey through Toronto's bike-friendly neighborhoods.

- Dedicated Bike Lanes: Toronto boasts an extensive network of dedicated bike lanes, providing a safe and efficient route for cyclists. Explore iconic neighborhoods such as Kensington Market or cruise along the waterfront trails with the city skyline as your backdrop.

- Bike-Share Programs: Take advantage of Toronto's bike-share programs, such as Bike Share Toronto. These programs allow users to rent bikes for short periods, making it easy to hop on and off at various locations around the city.

* **WALKING**:
- Pedestrian-Friendly Areas: Many neighborhoods in Toronto are pedestrian-friendly, featuring vibrant streets, shops, and cultural attractions. Stroll through iconic areas like Queen Street West, Yonge-Dundas Square, or the Distillery District to immerse yourself in the city's atmosphere.

- Waterfront Promenade: The Toronto waterfront offers a picturesque setting for a leisurely walk. Enjoy the serene views of Lake Ontario, explore the harborfront, or visit the Toronto Islands for a tranquil escape from the urban hustle.

- Guided Walking Tours: Join guided walking tours to discover Toronto's history, architecture, and hidden gems. Knowledgeable guides provide insights into the city's culture, making your walking experience both educational and entertaining.

* SAFETY AND ACCESSIBILITY:
   - Both biking and walking are embraced in Toronto, and safety measures, including pedestrian crossings and bike-friendly infrastructure, are integrated into the urban landscape. Many neighborhoods prioritize accessibility, making it easy for individuals of all abilities to enjoy these modes of transportation.

* PARKS AND GREEN SPACES:
   - Toronto is home to numerous parks and green spaces, offering scenic trails and pathways for walking and biking. High Park, the Toronto Beltline Trail, and the Martin Goodman Trail along the waterfront are just a few examples of the city's outdoor havens.

Whether you choose to pedal through the city streets or embark on a leisurely stroll, biking and walking in Toronto provide an intimate and engaging way to discover the city's charm. Embrace the freedom to explore at your own pace and savor the diverse landscapes that make Toronto a truly walkable and bike-friendly destination.

ACCOMMODATIONS

Toronto offers a diverse range of accommodations to suit every traveler's preferences, from luxurious hotels to budget-friendly options and unique stays. Whether you're seeking a central location in the heart of the city or a tranquil retreat, Toronto's lodging choices cater to a variety of tastes and needs.

HOTELS:

- Luxury Hotels: Experience opulence and top-notch service at Toronto's luxury hotels. From iconic establishments in the Financial District to stylish boutique options in Yorkville, these accommodations provide a lavish retreat with amenities like spa services, fine dining, and breathtaking city views.

- Mid-Range Options: Toronto boasts a plethora of mid-range hotels that balance comfort and affordability. Explore options in downtown areas like Queen Street West or the Entertainment District, offering convenient access to attractions and vibrant neighborhoods.

- Budget-Friendly Accommodations: Budget-conscious travelers can find a range of economical hotels and motels, particularly in areas like Kensington Market or the Annex. These accommodations provide a comfortable stay without compromising on accessibility.

ALTERNATIVE STAYS:

- Airbnb and Vacation Rentals: Enjoy a home-like experience by choosing an Airbnb or vacation rental. These options allow you to stay in residential neighborhoods, offering a taste of local life. Whether it's a cozy apartment or a spacious house, Toronto's diverse neighborhoods provide various choices.

- Boutique Inns: Discover unique boutique inns and guesthouses scattered throughout Toronto. These intimate accommodations often showcase distinctive decor and personalized service, providing a charming alternative to traditional hotels.

- Bed and Breakfasts: Experience warm hospitality at Toronto's bed and breakfast establishments. Located in residential areas or historic neighborhoods, these cozy accommodations offer a homely atmosphere and personalized service.

SPECIALTY STAYS:
  - Unique Hotels: Toronto features hotels with distinctive themes and designs. Whether it's a historic property with architectural significance or a hotel celebrating cultural diversity, these unique stays add an extra layer of character to your visit.

  - Extended Stay Options: For those planning a more extended visit, consider extended-stay hotels or serviced apartments. These accommodations provide additional amenities, such as fully equipped kitchens and laundry facilities, catering to a more independent style of living.

ACCESSIBILITY:
  - Toronto's accommodations prioritize accessibility, with many hotels featuring wheelchair-accessible rooms and facilities. When booking, it's advisable to communicate any specific accessibility requirements to ensure a comfortable stay.

As you plan your stay in Toronto, the city's diverse accommodations offer a wide spectrum of choices to enhance your travel experience. Whether you're looking for luxury, affordability, or a unique stay, Toronto's lodging options provide the perfect complement to your exploration of this dynamic city.

Hotels

Toronto offers a diverse range of hotels to cater to various preferences and budgets. For a luxurious stay, options like The Ritz-Carlton and Four Seasons Hotel provide opulent amenities and stunning views. Mid-range choices such as Thompson Toronto and Delta Hotels offer a blend of style and convenience. Budget-friendly accommodations like HI Toronto Hostel and Bond Place Hotel provide affordable options in central locations. Unique stays include The Drake Hotel for its artsy vibe and Gladstone Hotel with individual art-themed rooms. For a resort-like experience, Hotel X Toronto offers lakeside luxury. Whether seeking luxury, affordability, or a unique atmosphere, Toronto's hotels ensure a comfortable and memorable stay in this vibrant city.

Luxury Hotels

1. The Ritz-Carlton, Toronto

- Location: 181 Wellington Street West, Downtown Toronto
- Overview: An iconic luxury hotel in the heart of the city, The Ritz-Carlton Toronto offers a tranquil escape with a focus on personalized service.
- Room Types: Luxurious rooms and suites with upscale furnishings and stunning city or lake views.
- Amenities: Spa, TOCA restaurant, DEQ Lounge, fitness center, indoor pool, event spaces.
- Local Attractions: CN Tower, Roy Thomson Hall, Royal Ontario Museum.
- Booking Details: Reservations available on The Ritz-Carlton website or other online booking platforms.
- Price Range: Starting from $500 per night (varies by room type, season, and availability).

2. Four Seasons Hotel Toronto

- Location: 60 Yorkville Avenue, Yorkville Neighborhood
- Overview: The Four Seasons Hotel in Yorkville provides a refined and sophisticated atmosphere with a commitment to impeccable service.
- Room Types: Range of rooms and suites, some with private terraces and panoramic city views.
- Amenities: Spa, outdoor pool with terrace, Café Boulud, event spaces.
- Local Attractions: Yorkville shopping, Royal Ontario Museum, University of Toronto.
- Booking Details: Reservations can be made through the official Four Seasons website or other reputable booking platforms.
- Price Range: Starting from $600 per night (varies by room category, season, and availability).

These luxury hotels in Toronto offer a blend of sophistication and prime locations, ensuring a lavish and memorable stay for discerning travelers. Prices may vary based on factors such as room type, booking time, and seasonal demand.

Mid-Range Options

1. Thompson Toronto

- Location: 550 Wellington Street West, King West Village
- Overview: Thompson Toronto, situated in the trendy King West Village, offers a stylish stay with modern amenities and a rooftop pool.
- Room Types: Chic rooms with contemporary design and comfortable furnishings.
- Amenities: Rooftop pool, upscale dining, stylish ambiance.
- Local Attractions: Convenient access to entertainment districts and vibrant neighborhoods.
- Booking Details: Reservations available through the Thompson Toronto website or popular online booking platforms.
- Price Range: Mid-range pricing, with variations based on room type, season, and availability.

2. Delta Hotels Toronto

- Location: Multiple locations, including one near the CN Tower

- Overview: Delta Hotels offer contemporary accommodations with thoughtful amenities, making them suitable for both business and leisure travelers.
- Room Types: Comfortable rooms with modern furnishings and amenities.
- Amenities: Fitness center, on-site dining, event spaces.
- Local Attractions: Convenient access to attractions like the CN Tower and entertainment districts.
- Booking Details: Reservations can be made through the official Delta Hotels website or other reputable booking platforms.
- Price Range: Moderate pricing, with variations based on room category, season, and availability.

3. The Drake Hotel

- Location: 1150 Queen Street West, Queen Street West
- Overview: The Drake Hotel, located in the artsy Queen Street West neighborhood, offers a boutique stay with unique design and a lively atmosphere.

- Room Types: Artfully designed rooms with a creative touch.
- Amenities: On-site art installations, vibrant ambiance, live performances.
- Local Attractions: Proximity to the artistic and cultural scene of Queen Street West.
- Booking Details: Reservations available through The Drake Hotel website or popular online booking platforms.
- Price Range: Mid-range pricing, with variations based on room type, season, and availability.

These mid-range hotels in Toronto provide a balance of comfort and affordability, making them ideal for travelers seeking a stylish and convenient stay without breaking the budget. Prices may vary based on room type, booking time, and seasonal demand.

Budget–Friendly Accommodations

1. HI Toronto Hostel

- Location: 76 Church Street, Downtown Toronto
- Overview: HI Toronto Hostel provides budget-conscious travelers with a central location and a social atmosphere, making it

an ideal choice for those seeking economical options.

- Room Types: Shared and private rooms available for solo travelers or groups.
- Amenities: Communal spaces, kitchen facilities, organized activities for guests.
- Local Attractions: Convenient access to downtown attractions, theaters, and public transportation.
- Booking Details: Reservations can be made through the official HI Toronto Hostel website or popular online booking platforms.
- Price Range: Affordable pricing, with variations based on room type, season, and availability.

2. Bond Place Hotel

- Location: 65 Dundas Street East, Downtown Toronto
- Overview: Bond Place Hotel is a budget-friendly option located near Dundas Square, offering straightforward accommodations with modern amenities.
- Room Types: Comfortable rooms with essential amenities for budget-conscious travelers.

- Amenities: On-site restaurant, fitness center, convenient location.
- Local Attractions: Proximity to Dundas Square, shopping, and entertainment districts.

Booking Details: Reservations available through the Bond Place Hotel website or other reputable booking platforms.

Price Range: Affordable pricing, with variations based on room type, season, and availability.

These budget-friendly accommodations in Toronto provide practical and affordable options for travelers seeking a cost-effective stay in the city. Prices may vary based on room type, booking time, and seasonal demand.

Airbnb and Vacation Rentals

1. Airbnb

Location: Throughout Toronto, various neighborhoods

Overview: Airbnb offers a variety of accommodation options, from private rooms to entire apartments or houses, allowing travelers to experience a more local and personalized stay in different neighborhoods of Toronto.

Property Types: Diverse options, including apartments, houses, lofts, and unique stays.

Amenities: Vary depending on the property, often including kitchen facilities, local tips from hosts, and a more personalized experience.

Local Attractions: Depending on the chosen neighborhood, guests can enjoy proximity to local attractions, shops, and cultural sites.

Booking Details: Reservations can be made directly through the Airbnb platform, where hosts provide details on pricing, amenities, and house rules.

Price Range: Varied pricing, ranging from budget-friendly to higher-end options, depending on the property and location.

2. Vacation Rentals

- Location: Throughout Toronto, in various neighborhoods
- Overview: Vacation rentals, similar to Airbnb, offer a range of private accommodations. These rentals can include apartments, condos, or entire houses, providing flexibility for different travel preferences.
- Property Types: Apartments, condos, houses, and unique properties with varying amenities.

- Amenities: Fully furnished spaces, kitchen facilities, and the opportunity to experience local neighborhoods.
- Local Attractions: Depending on the location, vacation rentals provide access to nearby attractions, parks, and cultural sites.
- Booking Details: Reservations can be made through vacation rental platforms, each with its own booking process, including details on pricing, availability, and property features.
- Price Range: Variable pricing, with options suitable for different budgets and preferences.

3. Boutique Inns

- Location: Scattered throughout Toronto, often in residential or historic neighborhoods
- Overview: Boutique inns and guesthouses offer a unique and intimate lodging experience. These smaller establishments focus on personalized service and often feature distinctive decor.
- Property Types: Smaller inns and guesthouses with individually designed rooms.
- Amenities: Personalized service, unique decor, and a more intimate atmosphere.

- Local Attractions: Located in various neighborhoods, providing access to local attractions and cultural sites.
- Booking Details: Reservations can be made directly through the inn's website or popular booking platforms.
- Price Range: Variable pricing, often offering a balance between affordability and a unique experience.

These accommodation options, including Airbnb, vacation rentals, and boutique inns, provide travelers with a diverse range of choices for a more personalized and local experience in Toronto. Prices may vary based on the property type, location, and amenities offered.

Unique Stays

1. Gladstone Hotel

- Location: 1214 Queen Street West, Queen Street West
- Overview: The Gladstone Hotel is a boutique establishment in the artsy Queen Street West neighborhood, known for its unique design

and commitment to showcasing art and culture.

- Accommodation Types: Art-themed rooms with individual and distinctive decor.
- Amenities: On-site art installations, cultural events, and a vibrant atmosphere.
- Local Attractions: Proximity to the artistic and cultural scene of Queen Street West.
- Booking Details: Reservations can be made through the Gladstone Hotel website or popular online booking platforms.
- Price Range: Variable pricing based on room type, season, and availability.

2. The Anndore House

- Location: 15 Charles Street East, Yonge and Bloor- Overview: The Anndore House is a boutique hotel with a blend of modern and vintage aesthetics, located near the bustling intersection of Yonge and Bloor.
- Accommodation Types: Stylish rooms and suites with a unique design.
- Amenities: Contemporary decor, on-site dining, and a rooftop terrace.

- Local Attractions: Proximity to upscale shopping, cultural venues, and the University of Toronto.
- Booking Details: Reservations available through The Anndore House website or other reputable booking platforms.
- Price Range: Variable pricing based on room category, season, and availability.

3. Hotel X Toronto

- Location: 111 Princes' Boulevard, Exhibition Place
- Overview: Hotel X Toronto offers a resort-like experience with stunning views of Lake Ontario and the city skyline. It provides a blend of luxury and recreational amenities.
- Accommodation Types: Elegant rooms and suites with modern furnishings.
- Amenities: Rooftop pools, sports facilities, waterfront views, and multiple dining options.
- Local Attractions: Located near Exhibition Place, with easy access to lakeside attractions and events.

- Booking Details: Reservations can be made through the Hotel X Toronto website or popular online booking platforms.
- Price Range: Variable pricing based on room type, season, and availability.

These unique stays in Toronto offer travelers a distinctive and memorable experience, whether through art-themed rooms, boutique aesthetics, or resort-like amenities. Prices may vary based on room type, booking time, and seasonal demand.

WELCOME TO TORONTO

NEIGHBORHOODS

1. Downtown Toronto:

- Overview: The central hub of the city, Downtown Toronto is a bustling area with iconic landmarks like the CN Tower, entertainment districts, and the Financial District. It offers a mix of high-rise buildings, theaters, shopping, and cultural attractions.

2. Yorkville:

- Overview: Known for its upscale vibe, Yorkville is Toronto's premier shopping district with high-end boutiques, art galleries, and fine dining. The neighborhood also features beautiful Victorian homes and green spaces.

3. Queen Street West:

- Overview: A trendy and eclectic area, Queen Street West is a hub for arts, fashion, and indie culture. It's home to unique shops, street art, the Drake Hotel, and a vibrant nightlife scene.

4. Kensington Market:

- Overview: Kensington Market is a multicultural and bohemian neighborhood known for its diverse food scene, vintage shops, and colorful street art. It has a lively atmosphere and hosts various cultural events.

5. Distillery District:
- Overview: A historic area with cobblestone streets, the Distillery District is known for its preserved 19th-century buildings, art galleries, boutiques, and a wide array of cafes and restaurants.

6. The Annex:
- Overview: The Annex is a dynamic and student-friendly neighborhood near the University of Toronto. It features tree-lined streets, Victorian homes, cultural venues, and a mix of restaurants and bars.

7. Harbourfront:
- Overview: Located along Lake Ontario, Harbourfront offers picturesque waterfront views, parks, cultural venues like the Harbourfront Centre, and recreational activities. It's a popular spot for walking and cycling.

8. Leslieville:

- Overview: Leslieville is a hip and evolving neighborhood known for its artsy vibe, indie shops, and diverse dining options. It's a favorite among locals for its community feel and unique businesses.

9. Little Italy:

- Overview: Little Italy is a lively neighborhood with a strong Italian influence. It's famous for its authentic Italian restaurants, cafes, and cultural events. The vibrant atmosphere extends to College Street.

10. High Park:

- Overview: High Park is Toronto's largest public park, offering a retreat into nature within the city. It features hiking trails, a zoo, gardens, and a lake, providing a peaceful escape for residents and visitors.

11. Chinatown:

- Overview: Toronto's Chinatown is a dynamic and vibrant area with a rich cultural heritage. It's known for its diverse Asian cuisine, bustling markets, and cultural celebrations.

12. Liberty Village:

- Overview: Once an industrial area, Liberty Village has transformed into a trendy neighborhood with modern condos, tech offices, and a thriving arts and culture scene. It's known for its stylish boutiques and cafes.

Each neighborhood in Toronto has its unique charm, cultural influences, and attractions, making the city a mosaic of diverse experiences. Exploring these areas allows visitors to discover the richness and variety that Toronto has to offer.

Downtown Toronto

Overview:
Downtown Toronto is the beating heart of the city, encompassing a vibrant mix of business, culture, entertainment, and iconic landmarks. With a skyline dominated by sleek skyscrapers and a bustling atmosphere, this central district is a dynamic fusion of commerce and cultural richness.

Key Features:
1. CN Tower: A symbol of Toronto, the CN Tower offers breathtaking panoramic views of the city and beyond. Visitors can enjoy the Glass Floor, SkyPod,

and even an EdgeWalk around the tower's exterior for an adrenaline-pumping experience.

2. Financial District: Home to the city's major financial institutions and corporate offices, the Financial District is characterized by impressive high-rises and a bustling business atmosphere during weekdays.

3. Entertainment District: This lively area is a cultural hotspot, hosting theaters, live performances, and a vibrant nightlife scene. The Rogers Centre, home to the Toronto Blue Jays, and the Scotiabank Arena, a major sports and entertainment venue, are located here.

4. PATH Network: The PATH is an extensive underground pedestrian walkway, connecting various buildings, offices, and shopping centers. It's a haven during winter months and provides easy access to key locations.

5. Ripley's Aquarium of Canada: Located near the base of the CN Tower, this aquarium showcases marine life from around the world, featuring

interactive exhibits and a mesmerizing underwater tunnel.

6. Toronto Islands: A short ferry ride from Downtown, the Toronto Islands offer a peaceful escape with beaches, parks, and stunning views of the city skyline.

7. Royal Ontario Museum (ROM): Situated at the northern edge of Downtown, the ROM is Canada's largest museum, housing extensive collections of art, culture, and natural history.

Cultural Diversity:
Downtown Toronto reflects the city's multicultural identity, with a diverse range of restaurants, shops, and cultural events. Neighborhoods like Chinatown, Kensington Market, and Little Italy contribute to the rich tapestry of cultural experiences.

Shopping and Dining:
The downtown core is a shopping mecca, featuring flagship stores, designer boutiques on Bloor Street, and the historic Eaton Centre, one of North America's busiest shopping malls. The culinary

scene is equally diverse, offering everything from fine dining to international street food.

Accessibility:
Downtown Toronto is well-connected by public transportation, including the subway, streetcars, and buses. Union Station, a major transportation hub, facilitates regional and national rail travel.

Accommodations:
The area offers a range of accommodations, from luxury hotels with stunning city views to mid-range options and boutique stays. Visitors can choose accommodations that suit their preferences and provide easy access to key attractions.

Downtown Toronto, with its energy, cultural richness, and architectural marvels, invites visitors to explore its diverse offerings and experience the vibrant essence of Canada's largest city.

Entertainment District

Overview:
The Entertainment District in Toronto is a dynamic and lively neighborhood that serves as the cultural

epicenter of the city. Nestled in the heart of downtown, this district is synonymous with entertainment, featuring theaters, live performances, nightlife, and a vibrant urban atmosphere.

Key Features:

1. Theaters and Performing Arts: The Entertainment District is home to numerous theaters, including the Princess of Wales Theatre, Royal Alexandra Theatre, and the Ed Mirvish Theatre. These venues host a variety of Broadway-style productions, musicals, and live performances throughout the year.

2. Rogers Centre: An iconic sports and entertainment venue, the Rogers Centre is home to the Toronto Blue Jays baseball team. It also hosts major concerts, events, and international sports competitions. The stadium's retractable roof adds to its versatility.

3. Scotiabank Arena: This multi-purpose arena is a major hub for sports events, concerts, and entertainment shows. It is the home of the Toronto Maple Leafs (NHL) and the Toronto Raptors (NBA), drawing crowds for thrilling games and performances.

4. TIFF Bell Lightbox: The Toronto International Film Festival (TIFF) Bell Lightbox is a cultural institution dedicated to the art of cinema. It hosts film screenings, exhibitions, and events, attracting cinephiles and industry professionals.

5. Nightlife: The Entertainment District comes alive at night with an array of bars, clubs, and lounges. King Street West is particularly known for its vibrant nightlife, offering a diverse range of venues for music, dancing, and socializing.

6. CN Tower: While technically located just outside the district, the CN Tower is a prominent landmark visible from the Entertainment District. Its presence adds to the iconic skyline, and it often becomes part of the backdrop for events and performances in the area.

Cultural Diversity:
The district reflects Toronto's cultural diversity, with a mix of global cuisines, trendy bars, and international influences. Visitors can find everything from upscale dining establishments to casual eateries serving diverse culinary delights.

Accessibility:
The Entertainment District is easily accessible by public transportation, with subway stations, streetcar routes, and bus stops nearby. The district's central location makes it a convenient destination for both locals and tourists.

Accommodations:
Several hotels, ranging from luxury to mid-range, are scattered throughout the Entertainment District, offering convenient stays for those looking to immerse themselves in the vibrant atmosphere and cultural offerings.

The Entertainment District stands as a testament to Toronto's commitment to providing a rich and diverse array of entertainment options, making it a must-visit destination for those seeking a lively and culturally immersive experience in the city.

Distillery District

Overview:
The Distillery District is a unique and historic neighborhood located just east of downtown

Toronto. Known for its preserved 19th-century industrial architecture and cobblestone streets, this pedestrian-only district has been transformed into a cultural and entertainment hub.

Key Features:
1. Historic Ambiance: The Distillery District is characterized by its well-preserved red-brick Victorian industrial buildings. The cobblestone streets and heritage architecture create a charming and atmospheric setting reminiscent of the area's industrial past.

2. Art Galleries and Studios: The district is home to numerous art galleries, studios, and shops showcasing contemporary art and design. Visitors can explore exhibits, view public art installations, and even interact with artists in their studios.

3. Unique Shops and Boutiques: The Distillery District offers a diverse array of boutiques, specialty shops, and artisanal stores. Visitors can find unique fashion items, handmade crafts, and one-of-a-kind gifts, making it a shopping destination with a creative flair.

4. Cafés and Restaurants: The district boasts a variety of cafés, restaurants, and pubs, many housed in historic buildings. Whether enjoying a coffee on a sunny patio or indulging in a gourmet meal, visitors can savor a diverse culinary experience.

5. Performance Spaces: The area hosts live performances, including music, theater, and dance. The Distillery District is a cultural hotspot, with events and festivals taking place throughout the year, adding to the vibrant atmosphere.

6. Distillery Heritage Museum: Located within the district, the Distillery Heritage Museum provides insights into the area's history, showcasing artifacts and exhibits that highlight its evolution from a distillery to a cultural precinct.

Cultural Events:
The Distillery District is known for hosting cultural events and festivals, including the Toronto Christmas Market, which transforms the area into a festive wonderland during the holiday season. Various art and music festivals also take place, attracting both locals and tourists.

Accessibility:
While the Distillery District is a pedestrian-only area, it is easily accessible on foot from downtown Toronto. Visitors can enjoy a stroll through the district's cobblestone streets, explore its attractions, and experience the unique charm of the neighborhood.

Accommodations:
While there are no hotels within the Distillery District itself, there are accommodation options in the surrounding areas. Staying nearby allows visitors to easily explore the district's attractions on foot.

The Distillery District stands as a testament to Toronto's commitment to preserving and repurposing historic spaces, creating a unique blend of heritage, culture, and contemporary creativity for locals and visitors alike.

Kensington Market

Overview:
Kensington Market is a vibrant and eclectic neighborhood located to the west of downtown Toronto. Known for its bohemian atmosphere,

diverse community, and a kaleidoscope of colors, Kensington Market is a cultural hub that celebrates individuality, creativity, and a sense of community.

Key Features:

1. Diverse Culture and Community: Kensington Market is renowned for its cultural diversity and sense of community. The neighborhood is home to a mix of residents from various backgrounds, creating a unique and inclusive atmosphere.

2. Pedestrian-Friendly Streets: The streets of Kensington Market are pedestrian-friendly, allowing visitors to explore the area on foot. The narrow lanes are adorned with colorful street art, murals, and unique storefronts.

3. Vintage Shops and Boutiques: The market is a treasure trove for vintage enthusiasts and those seeking unique fashion finds. Vintage shops, boutiques, and thrift stores offer a wide array of clothing, accessories, and collectibles.

4. International Cuisine: Kensington Market is a food lover's paradise, with a diverse range of international cuisine. From hole-in-the-wall eateries

to trendy cafes, visitors can enjoy flavors from around the world, including Mexican, Caribbean, Middle Eastern, and more.

5. Artisanal and Specialty Shops: The market is dotted with artisanal shops, specialty stores, and independent businesses. Visitors can discover handmade crafts, locally produced goods, and unique items that reflect the creativity of local entrepreneurs.

6. Street Performers and Events: The streets of Kensington Market often come alive with the sounds of street performers, musicians, and artists. The neighborhood hosts events and festivals, adding to the lively and festive atmosphere.

Cultural Diversity:
Kensington Market's cultural richness is evident in its diverse offerings, from multicultural dining options to the unique expressions of art and fashion. The neighborhood is a melting pot of creativity and individuality.

Kensington Market Pedestrian Sundays:

During the warmer months, Kensington Market hosts "Pedestrian Sundays," where streets are closed to vehicular traffic, allowing pedestrians to freely explore and enjoy the vibrant street life, live performances, and outdoor markets.

Accessibility:
While parking is limited, Kensington Market is easily accessible by public transportation, including streetcars and buses. The area is also within walking distance from downtown Toronto.

Accommodations:
While there are no hotels within Kensington Market itself, there are accommodations available in nearby neighborhoods, allowing visitors to stay close to this lively and culturally rich area.

Kensington Market offers a unique blend of history, culture, and creativity, inviting visitors to immerse themselves in a neighborhood that celebrates diversity and individual expression.

Yorkville

Overview:

Yorkville is an upscale and chic neighborhood in Toronto, known for its sophisticated atmosphere, high-end shopping, fine dining, and luxurious residences. Located near the University of Toronto, this affluent district combines historic charm with modern elegance.

Key Features:
1. Boutique Shopping: Yorkville is a premier shopping destination, featuring designer boutiques, luxury brands, and upscale retailers. Bloor Street West, often referred to as the "Mink Mile," is lined with high-end fashion stores, making it a paradise for fashion enthusiasts.

2. Art Galleries and Museums: The neighborhood is home to several art galleries and cultural institutions. The Royal Ontario Museum (ROM), located at the northern edge of Yorkville, is one of the largest museums in North America, showcasing art, natural history, and cultural exhibits.

3. Fine Dining and Culinary Experiences: Yorkville offers an array of upscale dining options, from renowned restaurants to cozy cafés. Visitors can

indulge in gourmet cuisine, international flavors, and sophisticated dining experiences.

4. Luxury Hotels and Residences: The area boasts luxurious hotels and residences, providing an opulent stay for visitors. Some well-known hotels include The Four Seasons Hotel Toronto and The Hazelton Hotel, offering premium amenities and personalized service.

5. Yorkville Village: Formerly known as Hazelton Lanes, Yorkville Village is a shopping center that houses a mix of upscale boutiques, lifestyle stores, and fine dining establishments. It contributes to the area's reputation as a luxury shopping destination.

6. Cultural Events and Festivals: Yorkville hosts various cultural events and festivals throughout the year, attracting art enthusiasts and the fashionable elite. The neighborhood transforms during the Toronto International Film Festival (TIFF), bringing a glamorous and star-studded atmosphere.

Parks and Green Spaces:
Despite its urban setting, Yorkville offers green spaces for relaxation. The nearby Queen's Park and

the University of Toronto's campus provide tranquil areas for leisurely strolls and outdoor activities.

Cultural Diversity:
While Yorkville is known for its upscale offerings, it embraces cultural diversity, evident in its dining options, art scene, and the mix of residents and visitors from different backgrounds.

Accessibility:
Yorkville is easily accessible by public transportation, including the Toronto Transit Commission (TTC) subway system. The Bay Station and Museum Station provide convenient access to the neighborhood.

Accommodations:
Luxury hotels, boutique inns, and upscale residences cater to those seeking an indulgent stay in Yorkville. The accommodations reflect the neighborhood's commitment to providing an elevated and refined experience.

Yorkville stands as a symbol of sophistication in Toronto, where visitors can immerse themselves in a world of luxury, art, and culinary delights, creating an unforgettable experience in the heart of the city.

Leslieville

Overview:
Leslieville is a trendy and dynamic neighborhood located in the eastern part of Toronto. Known for its artistic vibe, diverse community, and eclectic mix of shops and eateries, Leslieville has evolved into a popular destination for locals and visitors seeking a unique and vibrant urban experience.

Key Features:
1. Artistic Community: Leslieville has a strong artistic community, with many galleries, studios, and street art installations. The neighborhood's creative spirit is reflected in its unique shops, boutiques, and the overall atmosphere.

2. Queen Street East: The main thoroughfare, Queen Street East, is the heart of Leslieville's commercial and cultural activity. It features a mix of independent shops, vintage stores, cozy cafes, and restaurants, contributing to the neighborhood's bohemian charm.

3. Culinary Scene: Leslieville is renowned for its diverse culinary offerings. From cozy brunch spots and trendy coffee shops to international cuisines and local eateries, the neighborhood caters to a range of palates.

4. Green Spaces: Residents and visitors can enjoy nearby parks and green spaces, including the beautiful Jimmie Simpson Park. These areas provide opportunities for outdoor activities, picnics, and a retreat from the urban bustle.

5. Unique Shops and Boutiques: Leslieville is home to a variety of unique shops and boutiques, offering everything from vintage clothing and antiques to handmade crafts and artisanal goods. It's a hub for those seeking one-of-a-kind finds.

6. Cultural Events: The neighborhood hosts various cultural events, markets, and festivals throughout the year. These events showcase local talent, foster a sense of community, and attract visitors looking for a lively and engaging experience.

Community Vibe:

Leslieville maintains a strong sense of community, with a mix of long-time residents, young professionals, and families. The neighborhood's welcoming atmosphere and diverse offerings contribute to its popularity as a place to live and explore.

Accessibility:
Leslieville is easily accessible by public transportation, with streetcar and bus routes connecting the neighborhood to downtown Toronto. The close proximity to major roadways also makes it convenient for those traveling by car.

Accommodations:
While there are no large hotels within Leslieville, visitors can find accommodations in nearby areas. Leslieville's charm often attracts those who prefer boutique hotels, bed and breakfasts, or vacation rentals.

Leslieville's vibrant and artistic character, combined with its welcoming community, makes it a unique and delightful destination within Toronto, offering a blend of creativity, culture, and urban flair.

TOP ATTRACTIONS

Toronto boasts a rich array of attractions that cater to diverse interests. The CN Tower stands tall as a symbol of the city, offering breathtaking views and adventurous experiences like the EdgeWalk. The Royal Ontario Museum (ROM) impresses with its vast collections spanning natural history and art, while the Art Gallery of Ontario (AGO) showcases a rich tapestry of Canadian and international artworks.

Ripley's Aquarium of Canada, located at the base of the CN Tower, immerses visitors in a mesmerizing underwater world. The Toronto Islands, accessible by a short ferry ride, provide a serene retreat with beaches and green spaces. The Distillery District, known for its historic charm, cobblestone streets, and cultural events, offers a unique and vibrant experience.

Kensington Market, a bohemian neighborhood, captivates with its eclectic shops, diverse eateries, and artistic flair. High Park, Toronto's largest public park, invites outdoor enthusiasts with walking trails, a zoo, and picturesque settings. Queen Street West, a trendy area, is a hub for fashion, art, and street life.

The Hockey Hall of Fame pays homage to the beloved sport, showcasing the history and achievements of hockey. Yonge-Dundas Square, often compared to Times Square, serves as a bustling public space surrounded by shopping, entertainment, and lively events.

These attractions collectively define Toronto's character, offering a blend of cultural richness, natural beauty, and vibrant urban experiences for both locals and visitors to enjoy.

CN Tower

Overview:
The CN Tower is an iconic landmark and a symbol of Toronto's skyline. Standing at 553.3 meters (1,815 feet), it held the title of the world's tallest freestanding structure for over three decades. Beyond its architectural significance, the CN Tower is a major tourist attraction, offering a range of experiences for visitors.

Key Features:

1. Panoramic Views: The CN Tower's observation decks provide unparalleled panoramic views of Toronto and the surrounding area. On a clear day, visitors can see as far as Niagara Falls and the shores of Lake Ontario.

2. Glass Floor and SkyPod: The tower features a Glass Floor, allowing brave visitors to step onto a transparent surface and look down at the city below. The SkyPod, situated even higher than the main observation deck, provides an elevated viewing experience.

3. EdgeWalk: For thrill-seekers, the CN Tower offers the EdgeWalk, an exhilarating experience where participants can walk on an outdoor platform encircling the tower's main pod at a height of 356 meters (1,168 feet).

4. Dining Options: The CN Tower houses two revolving restaurants, 360 Restaurant and Horizons Restaurant, offering not only fine dining but also a rotating view of the city. Visitors can enjoy a meal

while the restaurant slowly revolves, providing a unique dining experience.

Cultural Significance:
The CN Tower is deeply embedded in Toronto's cultural identity. It has been featured in numerous films, TV shows, and postcards, becoming an emblematic representation of the city. The tower's distinctive design and nighttime illumination contribute to Toronto's recognizable skyline.

Accessibility:
Located in the heart of downtown Toronto, the CN Tower is easily accessible by public transportation, including the PATH network. The area surrounding the tower is well-connected, making it a convenient destination for both locals and tourists.

Accommodations:
While there are no accommodations within the CN Tower itself, there are numerous hotels in the surrounding downtown area. Many of these hotels offer views of the CN Tower, providing guests with a unique perspective of this iconic structure.

The CN Tower remains a must-visit attraction, inviting individuals to experience Toronto from breathtaking heights, engage in thrilling activities, and appreciate the architectural and cultural significance of this iconic structure.

Royal Ontario Museum

Overview:

The Royal Ontario Museum (ROM) is Canada's largest museum and one of Toronto's premier cultural institutions. Located near the University of Toronto, the ROM is renowned for its diverse collections that span natural history, world cultures, and art, making it a compelling destination for visitors of all ages.

Key Features:

1. Exhibits and Galleries: The ROM houses a vast array of exhibits and galleries, showcasing artifacts and specimens from various disciplines. Notable exhibits include the Bat Cave, the dinosaur galleries, and the biodiversity displays.

2. Natural History: The natural history section of the ROM explores the world's natural wonders,

including fossils, minerals, gems, and taxidermy displays of various animal species. The dinosaur exhibits are particularly popular, featuring impressive dinosaur skeletons.

3. World Cultures: The ROM's World Cultures galleries highlight the rich diversity of human history and cultural practices. Visitors can explore artifacts from ancient civilizations, indigenous cultures, and contemporary societies.

4. Art Collections: The museum's art collections encompass a wide range of styles and periods, featuring paintings, sculptures, decorative arts, and textiles. The ROM's commitment to presenting art within a broader cultural context adds depth to its artistic displays.

5. Special Exhibitions: The ROM regularly hosts special exhibitions, showcasing a dynamic range of topics and collaborating with other museums worldwide. These temporary exhibits enhance the museum's offerings and attract visitors with diverse interests.

Cultural Significance:

The ROM plays a vital role in preserving and promoting Canada's cultural heritage. Its commitment to education and public engagement contributes to Toronto's identity as a hub of knowledge and cultural exploration.

Accessibility:
Situated in the heart of Toronto, the ROM is easily accessible by public transportation, including subway and bus services. Its central location makes it a convenient destination for both local residents and tourists exploring the city.

Educational Programs:
The ROM offers a variety of educational programs, workshops, and guided tours for visitors of all ages. These initiatives aim to enhance the learning experience and foster a deeper understanding of the museum's collections.

Architectural Significance:
The ROM's architecture is noteworthy, featuring a blend of historic and modern structures. The Michael Lee-Chin Crystal, an iconic addition designed by architect Daniel Libeskind, stands out

with its striking crystalline form, creating a modern contrast to the original building.

The Royal Ontario Museum stands as a cornerstone of Toronto's cultural landscape, inviting individuals to explore the wonders of the natural world, delve into diverse cultures, and engage with the dynamic exhibitions that define this esteemed institution.

Art Gallery of Ontario

Overview:
The Art Gallery of Ontario (AGO) is a prominent cultural institution located in downtown Toronto. Renowned for its extensive and diverse collection, the AGO is a hub for visual arts, housing works that span historical periods, cultural backgrounds, and artistic mediums.

Key Features:
1. Collections and Exhibits: The AGO's collections cover a wide spectrum of art, including European, Canadian, Indigenous, and contemporary works. Notable pieces include paintings by the Group of Seven, European masterpieces, and pieces by

renowned artists such as Emily Carr and Tom Thomson.

2. Canadian and Indigenous Art: The AGO is a significant custodian of Canadian and Indigenous art, featuring works that highlight the country's cultural diversity and artistic heritage. The Indigenous art collection includes pieces from various nations and time periods.

3. Henry Moore Sculpture Centre: The museum includes the Henry Moore Sculpture Centre, dedicated to the renowned British sculptor. The center displays a notable collection of Moore's sculptures and drawings, providing insight into his artistic evolution.

4. Special Exhibitions: The AGO regularly hosts special exhibitions, showcasing contemporary artists, thematic displays, and collaborations with other institutions. These exhibits contribute to the museum's dynamic programming and attract a diverse audience.

5. Walker Court: The central atrium of the AGO, known as Walker Court, is an architectural

masterpiece. The glass ceiling, designed by architect Frank Gehry, bathes the court in natural light and serves as a stunning focal point.

Community Engagement:
The AGO actively engages with the community through educational programs, workshops, and events. Initiatives like the AGO Youth Council and school programs aim to make art accessible to people of all ages and backgrounds.

Cultural Significance:
As a leading cultural institution, the AGO plays a crucial role in fostering artistic expression, preserving cultural heritage, and contributing to the city's vibrant cultural landscape. It reflects Toronto's commitment to supporting and celebrating the arts.

Accessibility:
Situated in downtown Toronto, the AGO is easily accessible by public transportation, including the subway and streetcar services. Its central location makes it a cultural hub for both locals and tourists exploring the city.

Architectural Features:

The AGO underwent a transformative expansion led by architect Frank Gehry. The redesign introduced modern elements, including the iconic glass and titanium façade, creating a visually striking addition to the historic building.

The Art Gallery of Ontario stands as a testament to Toronto's dedication to artistic expression and cultural enrichment, inviting visitors to immerse themselves in a world of creativity, diversity, and the beauty of the visual arts.

Ripley's Aquarium of Canada

Overview:
Ripley's Aquarium of Canada is a captivating aquatic attraction located near the base of the CN Tower in downtown Toronto. With a focus on marine life from around the world, the aquarium provides a mesmerizing and educational experience for visitors of all ages.

Key Features:
1. Underwater Tunnels: One of the highlights of the aquarium is the series of underwater tunnels that allow visitors to walk through acrylic tunnels

surrounded by water. This immersive experience provides unique views of marine life, including sharks, rays, and colorful fish.

2. Dangerous Lagoon: The Dangerous Lagoon is a central exhibit featuring a moving walkway through a massive underwater tunnel. It offers an up-close encounter with a variety of marine species, including sharks and sawfish, as they glide overhead.

3. Rainbow Reef: Rainbow Reef showcases a vibrant display of coral reefs and tropical fish. The exhibit recreates the beauty and diversity of underwater ecosystems, allowing visitors to explore the colorful world beneath the ocean's surface.

4. Touch Tanks: Ripley's Aquarium provides interactive touch tanks where visitors can touch and interact with various marine creatures, including rays and small sharks. These hands-on experiences add an educational element to the visit.

5. Jellyfish Exhibit: The mesmerizing Jellyfish Exhibit features these ethereal creatures in illuminated tanks, creating a visually stunning

display. The rhythmic movements of the jellyfish add to the tranquility of the exhibit.

6. Educational Programs: The aquarium offers educational programs, including guided tours, school programs, and sleepovers for a more immersive learning experience. These programs aim to promote marine conservation and awareness.

Cultural Significance:
Ripley's Aquarium of Canada contributes to Toronto's cultural landscape by providing an engaging and interactive space for learning about marine life. Its emphasis on conservation aligns with broader efforts to raise awareness about the importance of protecting the world's oceans.

Accessibility:
Situated in the heart of downtown Toronto, Ripley's Aquarium is easily accessible by public transportation, including the PATH network. Its central location makes it a popular destination for families, tourists, and school groups.

Family-Friendly Entertainment:

The aquarium caters to families with children, offering a range of activities and exhibits designed to captivate young minds. The interactive elements, colorful displays, and educational opportunities make it an ideal destination for family outings.

Ripley's Aquarium of Canada stands as a dynamic and engaging attraction, providing visitors with a glimpse into the wonders of the underwater world. Through its exhibits and educational initiatives, the aquarium encourages a deeper appreciation for marine life and the need for ocean conservation.

Toronto Islands

Overview:
The Toronto Islands are a collection of small islands located just off the downtown core of Toronto. This serene and picturesque archipelago in Lake Ontario offers a peaceful escape from the urban hustle, providing residents and visitors with a natural oasis.

Key Features:
1. Ferry Rides: Accessible by a short ferry ride, the Toronto Islands offer stunning views of the city skyline. The ferry journey itself provides a

refreshing transition from the bustling city to the tranquil island environment.

2. Centreville Amusement Park: Located on Centre Island, Centreville Amusement Park is a family-friendly attraction with rides, games, and a petting zoo. It adds a touch of whimsy to the islands and is a popular destination for children.

3. Beaches: The islands are known for their sandy beaches, including Hanlan's Point Beach, Centre Island Beach, and Ward's Island Beach. Visitors can relax by the water, enjoy a picnic, or engage in various water activities.

4. Biking and Walking Trails: The islands are crisscrossed with biking and walking trails, offering scenic routes through parks and wooded areas. Exploring the islands on foot or by bike provides an opportunity to appreciate the natural beauty and peaceful ambiance.

5. Toronto Island Park: The main green space on the islands, Toronto Island Park, features expansive lawns, gardens, and picnic areas. It's an ideal spot

for a leisurely stroll, family gatherings, or simply enjoying the outdoors.

6. Far Enough Farm: Situated on Centre Island, Far Enough Farm is a charming petting zoo with a variety of farm animals. It's a delightful attraction for families and those looking for a unique island experience.

Cultural Significance:
The Toronto Islands hold cultural significance as a recreational retreat and natural haven. Residents and visitors alike cherish the islands for their role in providing a peaceful escape and preserving green space within the city.

Conservation Efforts:
Efforts are ongoing to protect and conserve the natural habitats on the Toronto Islands. These initiatives aim to maintain the ecological integrity of the islands and ensure their sustainability for future generations.

Accessibility:
Ferries operate regularly from the Jack Layton Ferry Terminal, offering a convenient and scenic mode of

transportation to the islands. The islands are car-free, creating a pedestrian and cyclist-friendly environment.

Seasonal Events:
The Toronto Islands host various seasonal events, including the Toronto International Dragon Boat Race Festival and outdoor concerts. These events add vibrancy to the islands and attract a diverse range of visitors.

The Toronto Islands stand as a testament to the city's commitment to preserving natural spaces within an urban environment. Whether seeking outdoor recreation, family-friendly activities, or a peaceful retreat, the islands offer a diverse and rejuvenating experience just a short ferry ride away from downtown Toronto.

WELCOME TO TORONTO

CULTURAL EXPERIENCES

Toronto offers a rich tapestry of cultural experiences that captivate residents and visitors alike. The city's cultural landscape is characterized by a diverse range of artistic expressions, heritage celebrations, and immersive events.

The Royal Ontario Museum (ROM) stands as a cultural beacon, housing extensive collections that span natural history, world cultures, and art. Its exhibits provide a journey through time, exploring the depths of human history and the wonders of the natural world.

The Art Gallery of Ontario (AGO) contributes to Toronto's cultural vibrancy with its diverse art collections. From European masterpieces to contemporary works by Canadian and Indigenous artists, the AGO fosters appreciation for visual arts across various genres and styles.

For those seeking aquatic wonders, Ripley's Aquarium of Canada offers an immersive experience. Beyond its mesmerizing displays of marine life, the aquarium actively engages visitors in the importance of marine conservation, aligning cultural enrichment with environmental awareness.

The Toronto Islands provide a unique cultural experience by offering an escape from urban life. The islands, with their serene beaches, walking trails, and family-friendly attractions, serve as a natural sanctuary where cultural significance intertwines with the preservation of green spaces.

Cultural experiences extend beyond traditional institutions. Kensington Market, Leslieville, and Yorkville exemplify Toronto's neighborhoods as living canvases of cultural diversity. These areas celebrate individuality, creativity, and a sense of community, fostering unique expressions of art, cuisine, and lifestyle.

The Entertainment District and Distillery District showcase Toronto's commitment to cultural entertainment. The former pulsates with theaters, sports venues, and nightlife, while the latter preserves historic architecture and hosts cultural events, creating dynamic spaces for artistic expression.

Whether exploring the diverse neighborhoods, delving into the city's museums, or enjoying the tranquility of the Toronto Islands, cultural experiences in Toronto are an immersive journey through history, art, and the vibrant tapestry of the city's multicultural identity.

Theater and Performing Arts

Toronto's theater and performing arts scene is a dynamic and thriving community that showcases a diverse array of talent, productions, and venues. The city's commitment to the arts is evident in its numerous theaters, performance spaces, and a calendar filled with cultural events.

The Theater District, centered around King Street West, is a focal point for theatrical productions. Historic venues, such as the Royal Alexandra Theatre and the Princess of Wales Theatre, host Broadway and West End hits, attracting both local and international audiences. Mirvish Productions, a prominent theatrical production company, plays a key role in bringing world-class shows to Toronto.

The Four Seasons Centre for the Performing Arts is home to the Canadian Opera Company and the National Ballet of Canada. This architectural gem not only provides a world-class venue for opera and ballet but also contributes to the city's cultural richness.

The Sony Centre for the Performing Arts, with its iconic marquee, hosts a variety of performances, including concerts, dance productions, and Broadway shows. Its versatility makes it a hub for a wide range of artistic endeavors.

Smaller, independent theaters contribute to Toronto's vibrant arts community. The Factory Theatre, Tarragon Theatre, and Soulpepper Theatre Company are among the venues that showcase innovative and thought-provoking works, often featuring Canadian playwrights and emerging talents.

Every summer, the Toronto Fringe Festival takes over the city, bringing a flurry of independent and experimental performances to various venues. This festival celebrates the diversity of voices in the arts and provides a platform for emerging artists.

The Harbourfront Centre, situated along Lake Ontario, hosts cultural events and performances, including dance, music, and theater, with a focus on promoting diverse artistic expressions.

Toronto's commitment to inclusivity is evident in initiatives like the Native Earth Performing Arts, dedicated to showcasing Indigenous performing arts. The city's LGBTQ+ community is celebrated through events like Buddies in Bad Times Theatre, a world-renowned venue for queer theater.

The cultural mosaic of Toronto extends to its film festivals, with the Toronto International Film Festival (TIFF) standing as a global platform for cinematic excellence. The festival attracts filmmakers, actors, and cinephiles from around the world, solidifying Toronto's position in the international film scene.

In essence, Toronto's theater and performing arts scene is a dynamic and inclusive tapestry that reflects the city's commitment to cultural expression, diversity, and innovation. Whether in grand theaters or intimate venues, the performing arts play a vital role in shaping the cultural identity of this vibrant metropolis.

Music and Concerts

Toronto's music and concert scene is a dynamic and diverse tapestry that resonates with a wide range of genres, artists, and musical experiences. The city's vibrant music culture is showcased in its iconic venues, annual festivals, and a constant stream of live performances.

Iconic Venues:
Toronto boasts legendary venues that have become synonymous with the city's musical identity. The Massey Hall, with its historic charm, has hosted iconic performances spanning genres from jazz to rock. The Danforth Music Hall, a century-old venue, continues to host a mix of indie, rock, and electronic acts. The Horseshoe Tavern, known for its intimate atmosphere, has been a staple in the city's music scene for decades.

Concert Hubs:
The Entertainment District is a hub for concerts, with venues like the Scotiabank Arena hosting

international stars and major events. The Budweiser Stage, an outdoor amphitheater, provides a picturesque setting for summer concerts along the waterfront. Rebel, with its multi-room setup, caters to diverse musical tastes and electronic dance music enthusiasts.

Festivals:
Toronto's festivals showcase the city's musical diversity. The Toronto Jazz Festival brings world-class jazz performers to various stages, while the Beaches International Jazz Festival transforms the lakeside neighborhood into a musical celebration. NXNE (North by Northeast) and Canadian Music Week (CMW) are multi-venue festivals that highlight emerging and established artists across various genres.

Indie and Alternative Scene:
Toronto's indie and alternative music scene thrives in neighborhoods like Kensington Market and Queen Street West. The Cameron House, The Garrison, and Lee's Palace are venues that have nurtured independent and alternative acts, contributing to the city's reputation as a breeding ground for new musical talent.

Cultural Celebrations:
Ethnic neighborhoods like Little Italy, Greektown, and Chinatown host cultural celebrations that often feature live music, reflecting Toronto's multicultural fabric. These events provide a platform for diverse artists to showcase their talents and celebrate their cultural heritage.

Classical and Orchestral Performances:
The Toronto Symphony Orchestra, performing at Roy Thomson Hall, contributes to the city's classical music landscape. The Koerner Hall at the Royal Conservatory of Music hosts a variety of classical, jazz, and world music performances, attracting both local and international artists.

Street Performances:
Buskers and street performers add a touch of spontaneity to Toronto's music scene. Areas like Yonge-Dundas Square and the Distillery District often feature live performances, creating a lively atmosphere for both locals and tourists.

Indigenous Music Scene:

Toronto is a hub for Indigenous music, with organizations like the Indigenous Music Summit providing a platform for Indigenous artists to connect, collaborate, and showcase their talent.

In summary, Toronto's music and concert scene is a vibrant and ever-evolving mosaic that reflects the city's cultural diversity and passion for artistic expression. From world-renowned venues to grassroots initiatives, the city offers a musical journey that caters to every taste and preference.

Festivals and Events in 2024

Toronto's festivals and events calendar is a lively and diverse tapestry, reflecting the city's multicultural spirit, creativity, and enthusiasm for celebration. Throughout the year, Toronto comes alive with a myriad of events that cater to a wide range of interests and communities.

Toronto International Film Festival (TIFF):
TIFF stands as one of the world's most influential film festivals, attracting filmmakers, actors, and cinephiles from around the globe. The city transforms into a cinematic hub, showcasing

premieres, screenings, and industry events, contributing to Toronto's prominence in the international film scene.

Caribana Festival:
Celebrating the vibrant Caribbean culture, the Caribana Festival (officially known as the Toronto Caribbean Carnival) is a lively and colorful event. Parade processions, live music, and cultural performances take over the streets, offering a taste of Caribbean traditions and festivities.

Nuit Blanche:
Nuit Blanche is an annual contemporary art event that transforms the city into an open-air museum for one night. From dusk till dawn, art installations, performances, and exhibits pop up across Toronto, inviting residents and visitors to experience the city's creative energy in unexpected ways.

Toronto Pride Festival:
One of the largest Pride celebrations globally, the Toronto Pride Festival is a vibrant expression of LGBTQ+ pride and inclusion. The Pride Parade, cultural events, and performances create a festive

atmosphere, fostering community spirit and advocacy.

Toronto International Jazz Festival:
The Toronto Jazz Festival attracts jazz enthusiasts with its stellar lineup of local and international performers. Venues across the city host concerts, showcasing the diversity and improvisational spirit of jazz music.

Toronto International Festival of Authors (TIFA):
TIFA brings together authors, poets, and literary enthusiasts for a celebration of literature and storytelling. The festival features readings, discussions, and book signings, providing a platform for literary exchange.

Toronto Christmas Market:
Set in the historic Distillery District, the Toronto Christmas Market is a festive extravaganza that captures the spirit of the holiday season. Twinkling lights, artisanal crafts, and seasonal treats create a magical atmosphere for families and friends.

Canadian National Exhibition (CNE):

The CNE, also known as The Ex, marks the end of summer with a grand fair featuring amusement rides, live entertainment, and an array of food vendors. The airshow and nightly fireworks add to the excitement of this longstanding tradition.

Toronto International Festival of Dance (TIDF):
Dance enthusiasts converge during the TIDF, a showcase of diverse dance styles and choreographic works. Performances and workshops highlight the city's thriving dance community.

Toronto Beer Week:
Craft beer enthusiasts rejoice during Toronto Beer Week, an event that celebrates the city's burgeoning craft beer scene. Tastings, brewery tours, and beer-related events take place across Toronto.

From cultural celebrations to art exhibitions, Toronto's festivals and events offer a year-round kaleidoscope of experiences, fostering community engagement and showcasing the city's rich cultural tapestry.

Museums and Galleries

Toronto's museums and galleries contribute to the city's cultural richness, offering a diverse range of exhibits that span art, history, science, and cultural heritage. From world-class institutions to independent galleries, Toronto provides a dynamic and immersive experience for enthusiasts and visitors.

Royal Ontario Museum (ROM):
As Canada's largest museum, the ROM is a cultural icon in Toronto. Its extensive collections encompass natural history, world cultures, and art. The dinosaur exhibits, the Bat Cave, and the diverse cultural artifacts make the ROM a captivating destination for both education and entertainment.

Art Gallery of Ontario (AGO):
The AGO stands as a prominent cultural institution, housing an extensive collection of European, Canadian, Indigenous, and contemporary art. The museum's commitment to showcasing diverse artistic expressions and engaging exhibitions contributes to Toronto's reputation as a hub for the visual arts.

Ontario Science Centre:
A family-friendly destination, the Ontario Science Centre engages visitors with interactive exhibits that explore science, technology, and innovation. From hands-on experiments to immersive displays, the center fosters curiosity and learning for all ages.

Bata Shoe Museum:
The Bata Shoe Museum is a unique institution dedicated to the history, culture, and design of footwear. Its eclectic collection showcases footwear from various cultures and historical periods, offering a fascinating glimpse into the role of shoes in human history.

Aga Khan Museum:
Dedicated to Islamic art and culture, the Aga Khan Museum features a stunning collection of artifacts, manuscripts, and artworks. The museum's architecture and serene surroundings contribute to a contemplative and educational experience.

Gardiner Museum:
For those interested in ceramics and pottery, the Gardiner Museum is a specialized institution

highlighting the art and history of clay. Its exhibits, workshops, and events showcase the versatility and beauty of ceramic art.

Textile Museum of Canada:
Exploring the rich world of textiles, the Textile Museum of Canada features a diverse collection of textiles from various cultures and time periods. The museum's exhibits delve into the artistry, history, and cultural significance of textiles.

Museum of Contemporary Art (MOCA):
Located in the historic Junction neighborhood, MOCA showcases contemporary art with a focus on Canadian and Indigenous artists. The museum's innovative exhibits and programming contribute to Toronto's dynamic art scene.

Power Plant Contemporary Art Gallery:
Situated on the waterfront, the Power Plant is a leading contemporary art gallery presenting cutting-edge exhibitions by national and international artists. The gallery's commitment to experimental and thought-provoking art adds to Toronto's cultural landscape.

Small and Independent Galleries:
Toronto's artistic vibrancy extends to smaller galleries and independent art spaces. Areas like Queen Street West and Dundas Street West are home to a myriad of galleries, featuring works by emerging and established artists across various mediums.

Toronto's museums and galleries collectively provide a diverse and enriching cultural experience. Whether exploring the treasures of a major museum or discovering the avant-garde works in an independent gallery, the city offers a captivating journey through art, history, and cultural exploration.

SHOPPING IN TORONTO

Shopping in Toronto is a vibrant and diverse experience that caters to a wide range of tastes and preferences. The city is a shopping destination with everything from luxury boutiques and high-end fashion to eclectic markets and unique independent stores. Here's an overview of the shopping scene in Toronto:

Luxury Shopping:
Toronto boasts a thriving luxury shopping scene, especially in the Bloor-Yorkville area, often referred to as the Mink Mile. This upscale district features flagship stores of renowned international brands, including high-end fashion, jewelry, and designer boutiques. Holt Renfrew, a Canadian luxury department store, is a prominent fixture in this area, offering a curated selection of designer labels.

Queen Street West:
Known for its eclectic and artsy atmosphere, Queen Street West is a hub for independent boutiques, vintage shops, and unique fashion finds. This neighborhood embraces creativity, making it a

favorite among those seeking one-of-a-kind pieces and the latest trends from local designers.

Eaton Centre:
A shopping landmark in downtown Toronto, the Eaton Centre is one of the largest shopping malls in the city. With a vast array of retail stores, including major international brands and Canadian favorites, it provides a comprehensive shopping experience. The mall is also a popular destination for its diverse dining options.

Kensington Market:
For a bohemian and multicultural shopping experience, Kensington Market is the go-to destination. This pedestrian-friendly neighborhood is filled with independent shops, vintage stores, and unique vendors offering a variety of goods, from clothing to handmade crafts and international foods.

Yorkdale Shopping Centre:
Yorkdale Shopping Centre is another major mall in Toronto, known for its upscale offerings. It features a mix of luxury and mainstream brands, making it a sought-after destination for fashion enthusiasts. The

mall's contemporary design and diverse selection contribute to a premium shopping experience.

St. Lawrence Market:

For those interested in fresh produce, artisanal goods, and gourmet foods, St. Lawrence Market is a must-visit. This historic market, located in the Old Town neighborhood, offers a diverse range of vendors selling everything from local cheeses and meats to international delicacies.

Distillery District:

The Distillery District combines shopping with historic charm. Cobblestone streets are lined with boutiques, art galleries, and artisanal shops housed in restored Victorian-era buildings. Visitors can explore unique finds, including handmade jewelry, art, and specialty gifts.

Chinatown:

Toronto's vibrant Chinatown, centered around Dundas Street West and Spadina Avenue, is a bustling neighborhood filled with Asian markets, specialty stores, and unique boutiques. It's a fantastic destination for those looking for traditional Asian goods, herbs, and textiles.

Unique Neighborhoods:
Toronto's diverse neighborhoods each offer their own shopping flair. From the trendy shops of Leslieville to the upscale boutiques of Yorkville and the multicultural markets of Little Italy, exploring the various districts provides a range of shopping experiences.

In summary, shopping in Toronto is a dynamic and diverse adventure that caters to all tastes, from luxury seekers to those on the hunt for unique and locally crafted treasures. The city's mix of upscale malls, quirky neighborhoods, and cultural markets ensures that there's something for every shopper.

Yorkdale Shopping Centre

Overview:
Yorkdale Shopping Centre stands as one of Toronto's premier shopping destinations, renowned for its upscale offerings, diverse selection of brands, and contemporary design. Located in North York, this upscale shopping mall has consistently evolved to meet the changing preferences of shoppers while

maintaining a focus on luxury and high-end retail experiences.

Luxury and Upscale Brands:
Yorkdale is home to a prestigious collection of luxury and designer brands, including flagship stores for international fashion houses. Visitors can explore boutiques such as Gucci, Louis Vuitton, Prada, and Burberry, making it a destination for those seeking high-end fashion and accessories.

Fashion and Apparel:
The mall offers an extensive range of fashion and apparel options, catering to various tastes and styles. From popular international brands to Canadian designers, shoppers can find everything from casual wear to formal attire within the mall's diverse selection of stores.

Technology and Electronics:
Tech enthusiasts will appreciate the presence of cutting-edge technology and electronics stores at Yorkdale. Whether seeking the latest gadgets, smartphones, or home entertainment systems, the mall features reputable retailers specializing in technology and innovation.

Home and Lifestyle:
Yorkdale is not limited to fashion; it also boasts a variety of stores focusing on home and lifestyle. From upscale furniture to home decor and luxury kitchenware, the mall provides a curated shopping experience for those looking to enhance their living spaces.

Dining and Culinary Experiences:
Beyond shopping, Yorkdale offers a range of dining options, from casual eateries to upscale restaurants. Visitors can enjoy a diverse culinary experience, including international cuisines and gourmet offerings, making it a destination for both shoppers and food enthusiasts.

Services and Amenities:
The mall prioritizes customer experience, offering a range of services and amenities. These include personal shopping services, valet parking, and a concierge desk, enhancing the overall shopping experience for visitors.

Innovative Design and Atmosphere:

Yorkdale's design reflects a modern and sophisticated atmosphere. The mall's architecture incorporates natural light, open spaces, and contemporary aesthetics, creating an inviting environment for shoppers to explore and enjoy.

Seasonal Events and Promotions:
Throughout the year, Yorkdale hosts seasonal events, promotions, and exclusive launches. These initiatives contribute to the dynamic and evolving nature of the mall, providing additional incentives for visitors to explore new offerings.

Accessibility:
Yorkdale is easily accessible by both public transportation and car, with ample parking facilities. Its central location in North York makes it a convenient destination for locals and visitors alike.

In essence, Yorkdale Shopping Centre stands as a beacon of luxury retail in Toronto, offering a curated selection of upscale brands, fashion-forward boutiques, and a sophisticated shopping environment. The mall's commitment to providing a premium shopping experience has solidified its reputation as a destination for those seeking the epitome of style and quality.

Eaton Centre

Overview:
Toronto Eaton Centre, commonly referred to as Eaton Centre, is one of Canada's largest and most iconic shopping destinations. Located in the heart of downtown Toronto, this multi-level shopping mall attracts millions of visitors each year, offering a diverse range of retail stores, dining options, and entertainment experiences.

Retail Variety:
Eaton Centre houses a vast array of retail stores, ranging from international brands and flagship stores to Canadian favorites and specialty shops. Visitors can explore fashion, electronics, beauty products, home goods, and much more, providing a comprehensive shopping experience under one roof.

Flagship Stores:
The mall is home to several flagship stores, making it a destination for exclusive and sought-after products. Popular brands such as Apple, Samsung,

Nordstrom, and Uniqlo have flagship locations within Eaton Centre, showcasing their latest innovations and collections.

Fashion and Apparel:
Eaton Centre is a fashion hub, featuring a wide selection of clothing stores catering to various styles and budgets. From trendy fast-fashion retailers to upscale boutiques, shoppers can find a diverse range of fashion options for men, women, and children.

Dining and Culinary Experiences:
The diverse dining options at Eaton Centre cater to various tastes and preferences. Whether seeking a quick bite at the food court or a leisurely meal at a sit-down restaurant, visitors can enjoy a culinary journey featuring international cuisines and local favorites.

Entertainment and Amenities:
Beyond shopping and dining, Eaton Centre offers entertainment options and amenities. The mall hosts events, performances, and seasonal promotions, providing additional attractions for visitors. Services such as personal shopping, beauty salons, and tech

support contribute to a well-rounded shopping experience.

Architectural Icon:
Eaton Centre is known for its distinctive architecture, particularly the iconic glass-domed galleria known as the "Flight Stop." This architectural feature adds a sense of grandeur and natural light to the mall's interior, creating a unique and inviting atmosphere.

Accessibility:
Situated in downtown Toronto, Eaton Centre is easily accessible by public transportation, including the subway and bus services. Its central location makes it a convenient destination for both locals and tourists exploring the city.

Integration with the City:
Eaton Centre is seamlessly integrated into the urban fabric of Toronto. Its location connects it to the city's financial district, theaters, and cultural institutions, making it a central hub for both shopping and urban exploration.

Seasonal Decor and Events:

Eaton Centre embraces seasonal themes, with elaborate decorations and events during holidays and special occasions. The mall's festive atmosphere adds to the overall shopping experience and creates a sense of celebration.

In summary, Toronto Eaton Centre stands as a landmark shopping destination, offering a comprehensive retail experience, a diverse range of dining options, and a unique architectural ambiance. Its central location and integration with the city's cultural and business districts make it a bustling and iconic part of Toronto's urban landscape.

Queen Street West

Overview:
Queen Street West is a vibrant and eclectic neighborhood in Toronto known for its diverse culture, artistic flair, and unique shopping scene. Stretching from University Avenue to Roncesvalles Avenue, this bustling street is a hub for independent boutiques, trendy shops, artistic spaces, and a dynamic mix of culinary experiences.

Independent Boutiques and Fashion:
Queen Street West is renowned for its independent boutiques and cutting-edge fashion offerings. The neighborhood is a haven for those seeking unique and trendy clothing, accessories, and lifestyle items. Local designers and emerging brands often set up shop here, contributing to the area's reputation as a fashion-forward district.

Art Galleries and Studios:
The street is dotted with art galleries and studios, showcasing Toronto's contemporary art scene. From avant-garde exhibitions to street art murals, Queen Street West celebrates creativity, making it a must-visit for art enthusiasts and those looking to explore the city's cultural landscape.

Vintage and Retro Finds:
Vintage and retro enthusiasts will find a treasure trove of shops along Queen Street West. These stores offer curated collections of vintage clothing, accessories, vinyl records, and unique retro items. The area's retro charm and nostalgic vibes attract a diverse crowd of shoppers.

Culinary Delights:

Queen Street West is a culinary destination with a diverse range of restaurants, cafes, and eateries. From trendy brunch spots to international cuisine and innovative food concepts, the street caters to various tastes. The culinary scene is known for its creativity and emphasis on local, fresh ingredients.

Live Music and Entertainment:
The neighborhood comes alive with live music venues, creating a vibrant atmosphere for music enthusiasts. From intimate indie performances to larger concert spaces, Queen Street West offers a dynamic music scene that contributes to Toronto's reputation as a music hub.

Cultural Hotspots:
Cultural institutions such as the Museum of Contemporary Art (MOCA) contribute to the neighborhood's artistic vibrancy. MOCA, located on Sterling Road just off Queen Street West, showcases contemporary art exhibitions and installations.

Pedestrian-Friendly Atmosphere:
The street features wide sidewalks, creating a pedestrian-friendly environment. Outdoor patios, street art installations, and pop-up markets add to the

street's dynamic and inviting atmosphere. The pedestrian-friendly design encourages leisurely strolls and exploration.

Festivals and Events:
Queen Street West hosts various festivals and events throughout the year. From art festivals to fashion shows and street celebrations, the neighborhood's events contribute to its lively and inclusive community spirit.

Nightlife:
As the sun sets, Queen Street West transforms into a lively nightlife destination. Bars, pubs, and clubs offer diverse atmospheres, from laid-back spaces for craft beer enthusiasts to energetic venues for those seeking a night of dancing and entertainment.

Local Markets:
Seasonal markets and pop-up shops further enhance the neighborhood's shopping experience. These markets showcase handmade goods, local artisans, and unique finds, adding to the area's reputation as a hub for independent and creative businesses.

In summary, Queen Street West is a dynamic and culturally rich neighborhood in Toronto, offering a blend of artistic expression, unique shopping experiences, and a diverse culinary scene. Whether exploring the boutiques, enjoying live music, or discovering local art, Queen Street West provides a vibrant and authentic taste of Toronto's creative spirit.

Distillery District Shops

The Distillery District is a historic and charming neighborhood in Toronto renowned for its cobblestone streets, preserved Victorian-era architecture, and a vibrant mix of shops, galleries, and artisanal boutiques. The pedestrian-friendly area is a unique shopping destination that blends history with contemporary craftsmanship. Here's an overview of some of the distinctive shops you can find in the Distillery District:

Art Galleries:
The Distillery District is home to numerous art galleries showcasing a diverse range of contemporary and traditional artworks. Local and international artists often display their paintings,

sculptures, and multimedia installations, providing visitors with a chance to immerse themselves in the thriving art scene.

Artisanal Boutiques:
Many shops in the Distillery District specialize in artisanal and handcrafted goods. Visitors can explore boutiques offering unique items such as handmade jewelry, textiles, ceramics, and leather goods. These artisanal shops emphasize craftsmanship and individuality, providing an alternative to mass-produced goods.

Home Decor and Design Stores:
For those looking to enhance their living spaces, the Distillery District features home decor and design stores. From vintage furniture and eclectic pieces to modern designs, these shops curate a collection of items that add character to homes.

Fashion Boutiques:
Fashion enthusiasts can explore boutiques in the Distillery District that showcase curated selections of clothing, accessories, and footwear. Whether seeking trendy and contemporary fashion or timeless

pieces with a unique twist, the district offers a range of options.

Gourmet and Specialty Food Shops:
Food lovers will appreciate the gourmet and specialty food shops scattered throughout the district. These establishments offer a delightful array of artisanal chocolates, locally crafted olive oils, gourmet spices, and other culinary delights. It's a perfect place to find unique gifts for foodies.

Unique Gift Shops:
The Distillery District is known for its unique gift shops where visitors can find one-of-a-kind souvenirs and presents. These shops often feature items crafted by local artisans, ensuring a distinctive and memorable shopping experience.

Antique Stores:
For those with a penchant for vintage finds and antique treasures, the Distillery District has antique stores that showcase carefully curated collections of furniture, decor items, and nostalgic pieces from the past.

Specialty Craft Shops:

Craft enthusiasts can explore specialty shops that focus on various crafts and hobbies. Whether it's knitting supplies, handmade soap, or specialty teas, these shops cater to those who appreciate the art of crafting.

Bookstores and Literary Spaces:
The district also boasts bookstores and literary spaces, providing a cozy environment for book lovers to explore a curated selection of titles. Some stores may specialize in rare or independent publications, offering a unique browsing experience.

Bespoke and Custom Shops:
Certain shops in the Distillery District offer bespoke and custom-made products. Whether it's personalized jewelry, tailored clothing, or custom artwork, these shops provide an opportunity for visitors to own something truly unique.

In summary, the Distillery District's shops contribute to its character as a hub for artistic expression, craftsmanship, and unique retail experiences. Whether exploring art galleries, discovering handcrafted goods, or indulging in gourmet treats, visitors can immerse themselves in the rich tapestry of the Distillery District's shopping scene.

DINING AND CUISINE

Toronto's dining scene is a culinary voyage through global flavors, reflecting the city's diverse cultural landscape. From bustling food markets to fine dining establishments, Toronto offers a gastronomic adventure for every palate. Explore the ethnic enclaves like Chinatown and Little Italy, where authentic dishes transport you to far-off lands. The city's food markets, including St. Lawrence Market, are a sensory delight, showcasing fresh produce, artisanal goods, and delectable treats. Indulge in international cuisines, from sushi in the Entertainment District to Indian delights in Gerrard India Bazaar. Toronto's commitment to farm-to-table practices is evident in its thriving food culture, with chefs incorporating local, seasonal ingredients into their creations. Whether you're savoring a classic Canadian dish like poutine or diving into a fusion culinary experience, Toronto's dining scene is a tapestry of flavors waiting to be explored.

Iconic Toronto Foods

Toronto boasts a delectable array of iconic foods that capture the essence of the city's diverse culinary landscape. From savory classics to sweet delights, these dishes have become synonymous with the Toronto food experience.

Peameal Bacon Sandwich:
A Toronto staple, the peameal bacon sandwich features peameal bacon, also known as back bacon, served on a bun. Often adorned with mustard, this sandwich is a breakfast favorite.

Butter Tart:
A quintessentially Canadian dessert, the butter tart has a gooey, buttery filling encased in a flaky pastry shell. Variations may include pecans or raisins.

Poutine:
Originating from Quebec but embraced across Canada, poutine is a comfort food favorite. Crispy fries are topped with cheese curds and smothered in savory gravy.

Toronto-Style Pizza:
Toronto's pizza scene is distinct, featuring a style that combines various influences. Often characterized by a thin crust, generous toppings, and a unique blend of flavors.

Kensington Market's Global Eats:
Kensington Market is a culinary melting pot, offering diverse street foods from around the world. Explore Jamaican patties, tacos, dumplings, and more.

Jerk Chicken:
A nod to Toronto's vibrant Caribbean community, jerk chicken is a flavorful and spicy dish that reflects the city's multicultural influences.

Toronto Sushi Rolls:
Toronto has its own take on sushi, with inventive rolls that often incorporate non-traditional ingredients. The city's sushi scene is a fusion of Japanese flavors with local twists.

Bannock:
Bannock, a traditional Indigenous bread, has found its way into Toronto's culinary scene. Enjoy it as a side or in creative variations, such as bannock tacos.

BeaverTails:
A beloved Canadian treat, BeaverTails are pastries stretched into the shape of a beaver's tail, deep-fried

to golden perfection, and topped with various sweet toppings.

Toronto-Style Hot Dog:
Found at hot dog stands throughout the city, the Toronto-style hot dog often features a diverse array of toppings, including sautéed onions, relish, and mustard.

These iconic Toronto foods reflect the city's rich cultural tapestry and are must-tries for anyone looking to savor the unique flavors that define Toronto's culinary identity.

Fine Dining Restaurants

Toronto's fine dining scene is a culinary journey that combines exquisite flavors, impeccable service, and elegant ambiance. The city is home to a diverse array of fine dining establishments, each offering a unique gastronomic experience. Here are a few noteworthy fine dining restaurants in Toronto:

1. Alo:
Alo consistently ranks among Toronto's best fine dining establishments. With a French-inspired

tasting menu, Alo offers an intimate and sophisticated dining experience. The restaurant's attention to detail and culinary artistry make it a destination for food enthusiasts.

2. Canoe:

Perched atop the TD Bank Tower, Canoe provides not only exquisite Canadian cuisine but also breathtaking views of the city skyline. Known for its seasonal and locally sourced menu, Canoe elevates Canadian ingredients into culinary masterpieces.

3. George Restaurant:

Located in a historic building in downtown Toronto, George Restaurant is known for its modern Canadian cuisine. The ever-evolving tasting menu showcases innovative dishes crafted with precision and creativity.

4. Scaramouche Restaurant:

Overlooking the city from its perch on the 38th floor, Scaramouche Restaurant offers French-inspired cuisine with a focus on fresh, high-quality ingredients. The restaurant is celebrated for its elegant atmosphere and impeccable service.

5. Edulis:

Edulis is a gem in Toronto's culinary landscape, specializing in seasonal and foraged ingredients. The intimate setting, coupled with a menu that changes daily, creates a dining experience that is both adventurous and refined.

6. Bosk at Shangri-La Hotel:

Bosk, located in the Shangri-La Hotel, is renowned for its contemporary and globally influenced menu. The restaurant's chic ambiance, coupled with its commitment to culinary excellence, makes it a sought-after destination for fine dining enthusiasts.

7. Canis Restaurant:

Canis is known for its minimalist yet artful approach to cuisine. The ever-changing tasting menu showcases a commitment to local and seasonal ingredients, creating a dining experience that is both adventurous and sophisticated.

8. Auberge du Pommier:

Nestled in a historic cottage, Auberge du Pommier offers a refined French dining experience. The restaurant's classic yet innovative dishes, complemented by an extensive wine list, make it a perennial favorite.

9. TOCA at The Ritz-Carlton:
TOCA combines Italian-inspired cuisine with a luxurious setting at The Ritz-Carlton. The restaurant features a diverse menu with an emphasis on fresh, house-made ingredients.

10. The Civic at The Broadview Hotel:
- Housed in a beautifully restored historic building, The Civic at The Broadview Hotel offers modern Canadian cuisine with a focus on local and seasonal ingredients. The restaurant's elegant setting adds to the overall fine dining experience.

These fine dining establishments represent just a glimpse into Toronto's vibrant culinary scene, where culinary innovation and culinary excellence converge to create memorable dining experiences.

Street Food and Food Markets

Toronto's street food scene and food markets offer a diverse and vibrant culinary experience, reflecting the city's rich cultural tapestry. From bustling food markets to food trucks, these culinary hubs showcase an array of flavors and global influences.

Street Food

Food Trucks:
Toronto's streets are alive with a dynamic array of food trucks, each offering a unique culinary experience. From gourmet grilled cheese to international delights like tacos and falafel, these mobile kitchens cater to a variety of tastes.

Chinatown Street Snacks:
Exploring Toronto's Chinatown, particularly along Spadina Avenue, reveals a treasure trove of street food. Indulge in steamed buns, bubble tea, dim sum, and other savory and sweet Asian treats.

Kensington Market Eats:
Kensington Market is a bohemian enclave with a lively street food scene. Wander through its narrow streets to discover diverse offerings, including empanadas, jerk chicken, and an eclectic array of global street snacks.

Food Markets

St. Lawrence Market:
A Toronto culinary institution, St. Lawrence Market is a mecca for food enthusiasts. Explore its stalls filled with fresh produce, artisanal cheeses, meats, and prepared foods. Don't miss out on the iconic peameal bacon sandwiches and butter tarts.

Distillery District Food Market:
Periodic food markets in the Distillery District bring together local vendors and food artisans. These markets offer a diverse selection of gourmet delights, from artisanal chocolates to unique street food.

Front Street Foods at Union Station:
Located at Union Station, Front Street Foods is a seasonal market featuring a curated selection of food vendors. It's an excellent spot to grab a quick bite while experiencing the city's culinary diversity.

Market 707:
Situated at Scadding Court Community Centre, Market 707 is an outdoor market composed of repurposed shipping containers turned into food

stalls. It offers a multicultural array of global street foods.

Evergreen Brick Works Farmers Market:
The weekly farmers market at Evergreen Brick Works showcases local vendors offering fresh produce, artisanal goods, and ready-to-eat treats. It's a hub for sustainable and locally sourced products.

Toronto Food Truck Festival:
The Toronto Food Truck Festival, held annually, gathers a diverse selection of food trucks, providing a feast for food lovers. It's a celebration of culinary creativity on wheels.

Toronto Night Market:
The Toronto Night Market at 1 Spadina Crescent is a lively event featuring diverse vendors, live entertainment, and an eclectic mix of global street food. It transforms the night into a culinary adventure.

Exploring Toronto's street food and food markets is not just about satiating hunger; it's an immersive journey into the city's multicultural identity and a celebration of its culinary diversity. From savory bites to sweet indulgences, these culinary destinations offer a taste of Toronto's vibrant food culture.

Vegetarian and Vegan Options

Toronto's culinary landscape embraces the growing demand for vegetarian and vegan options, offering a diverse array of plant-based dishes. Whether you're a dedicated vegan or just exploring a meatless lifestyle, Toronto has a variety of options to suit every taste. Here are some standout vegetarian and vegan options in the city:

1. Fresh Restaurants:
Fresh Restaurants are renowned for their creative and diverse plant-based menu. From hearty bowls to innovative salads, Fresh offers a range of options in a casual and vibrant setting.

2. Planta:
Planta is an upscale vegan restaurant that redefines plant-based dining. With a focus on elevated and beautifully presented dishes, Planta showcases the culinary possibilities of a vegan menu.

3. Doomie's:
Doomie's is a comfort food haven for vegans, serving indulgent and satisfying plant-based versions of classic dishes. From burgers to mac 'n' cheese, Doomie's proves that vegan comfort food is both flavorful and hearty.

4. Hogtown Vegan:
Hogtown Vegan specializes in vegan comfort food with a Southern twist. From crispy "chicken" sandwiches to BBQ "ribs," this spot offers a flavorful journey into vegan comfort cuisine.

5. Urban Herbivore:
Urban Herbivore is a vegetarian and vegan-friendly eatery known for its fresh salads, wraps, and bowls. With a focus on wholesome ingredients, it caters to those seeking light and nutritious options.

6. Grasshopper Restaurant:
Grasshopper Restaurant offers a diverse menu of vegan Asian-inspired dishes. From noodle bowls to sushi rolls, it's a go-to spot for those craving plant-based flavors with an international flair.

7. Kupfert & Kim:

Kupfert & Kim is a quick-service restaurant with a focus on nutrient-dense, plant-based meals. Their menu includes grain bowls, salads, and breakfast options, all crafted with a commitment to sustainability.

8. Apiecalypse Now!:

Apiecalypse Now! is a vegan bakery and pizzeria that serves up delicious plant-based pizzas, pastries, and savory treats. It's a haven for those with a sweet tooth and a love for vegan pizza.

9. Veghed:

Veghed offers a menu centered around plant-based comfort food. From vegan poutine to loaded nachos, it's a spot where indulgence meets compassionate dining.

10. Rosalinda:

- Rosalinda is a chic and vibrant vegan restaurant with a menu inspired by Mexican flavors. The restaurant's stylish setting complements its diverse and flavorful plant-based dishes.

These establishments represent just a glimpse of Toronto's thriving vegetarian and vegan scene.

Whether you're seeking a quick bite, a fine dining experience, or comfort food with a plant-based twist, Toronto has a wealth of options to cater to every palate and preference.

NIGHTLIFE

Toronto's nightlife is a dynamic and diverse scene that caters to a wide range of preferences. The Entertainment District, particularly along King Street West, stands out as a bustling hub with a mix of upscale lounges, high-energy nightclubs, and live music venues. Queen Street West, known for its artistic flair, transforms into a vibrant nightlife destination with indie bars and creative spaces.

Rooftop bars across the city offer stunning views of the skyline, providing an upscale and sophisticated atmosphere. Live music enthusiasts can explore iconic venues like The Danforth Music Hall and Lee's Palace, where local and international artists showcase their talents.

The Distillery District, with its historic charm, becomes an enchanting evening destination featuring candlelit patios and artisanal cocktail lounges. The LGBTQ+ community finds a welcoming space in the Church-Wellesley Village, home to energetic clubs and drag performances.

Late-night eateries and 24-hour diners cater to those seeking post-party sustenance. Cultural hotspots like the Royal Ontario Museum and the Art Gallery of Ontario occasionally host themed nights, offering unique experiences for those interested in art and history.

Throughout the neighborhoods, from the trendy King Street West to the local gems in various districts, Toronto's nightlife weaves a vibrant tapestry. Whether enjoying the lively atmosphere of the Entertainment District, exploring hidden gems in Queen Street West, or savoring late-night bites, the city's nightlife ensures there's something for everyone as the sun sets.

Bars and Pubs

Toronto boasts a diverse and vibrant bar and pub scene, offering a wide range of options for those looking to enjoy a night out. Here's an overview of the city's bars and pubs:

Entertainment District Bars:
The Entertainment District is a bustling hub for nightlife, housing an array of bars and clubs.

Whether you're into chic lounges, rooftop bars with scenic views, or high-energy dance clubs, this area has options to suit various tastes. Notable venues include Cube, Wildflower, and Lavelle.

King Street West Lounges:
King Street West is lined with upscale lounges that cater to a sophisticated crowd. These venues often feature craft cocktails, stylish decor, and an ambiance perfect for intimate gatherings. Baro, Bisha Hotel's KOST, and Thompson Hotel's Lobby Bar are popular choices.

Queen Street West Indie Bars:
Queen Street West, known for its artsy vibe, offers a mix of indie bars and pubs. These venues often showcase live music, local artists, and a laid-back atmosphere. The Cameron House and The Horseshoe Tavern are iconic spots for live music enthusiasts.

Rooftop Bars:
Toronto's skyline provides a picturesque backdrop for rooftop bars. These venues offer a combination of stunning views, craft cocktails, and a trendy

atmosphere. The Broadview Hotel Rooftop and Kost are among the rooftop gems in the city.

Distillery District Pubs:
The Distillery District, while known for its historic charm, also houses cozy pubs and bars. These establishments often feature a selection of craft beers, classic pub fare, and a relaxed ambiance. El Catrin and Mill Street Brew Pub are favorites in this district.

Neighborhood Pubs:
Toronto's neighborhoods have their own local pubs, providing a sense of community and a more laid-back atmosphere. These pubs often serve a variety of beers on tap and may feature pub quizzes or live sports screenings. The Local, Betty's, and The Wallace are examples of neighborhood favorites.

Craft Beer Bars:
For beer enthusiasts, Toronto offers a thriving craft beer scene with bars specializing in a diverse range of local and international craft brews. Bar Hop, C'est What, and Bellwoods Brewery are popular

destinations for those looking to explore unique beer selections.

Irish Pubs:

The city is home to traditional Irish pubs that offer a cozy atmosphere, hearty pub grub, and a selection of Irish and local beers. Quinn's Steakhouse & Irish Bar and The Auld Spot Pub are well-known Irish establishments in Toronto.

LGBTQ+ Bars:

Church-Wellesley Village is the epicenter of Toronto's LGBTQ+ community and features a variety of LGBTQ+ bars. Woody's, Crews & Tangos, and Buddies in Bad Times Theatre offer inclusive spaces with lively entertainment.

Sports Bars:

For sports enthusiasts, Toronto has numerous sports bars where you can catch the latest game on big screens. Real Sports Bar & Grill, The Loose Moose, and Wayne Gretzky's are popular choices for sports viewing.

In summary, Toronto's bars and pubs cater to a diverse audience, providing everything from upscale lounges to neighborhood pubs, rooftop bars to craft beer havens. Whether you're seeking live music, a scenic view, or a cozy spot for a pint, the city's nightlife offers a plethora of options to explore.

Nightclubs

Toronto's nightlife is renowned for its energetic and diverse nightclub scene, drawing partygoers with a variety of music, atmospheres, and experiences. Here's an overview of some of the notable nightclubs in the city:

Uniun Nightclub:
Located in the Entertainment District, Uniun is a visually stunning nightclub known for its immersive lighting, state-of-the-art sound system, and a spacious dance floor. The venue hosts a mix of electronic dance music (EDM) events and top-notch DJ performances.

REBEL:
Formerly known as Sound Academy, REBEL is one of Toronto's largest and most iconic nightclubs. Situated on the waterfront, REBEL boasts multiple rooms with diverse music genres, high-end

production, and a vibrant atmosphere. It often hosts internationally renowned DJs and live performances.

Coda:
Coda is a popular destination for electronic music enthusiasts. This intimate nightclub in the Annex neighborhood features a Funktion-One sound system and hosts both local and international DJs, making it a favorite for techno and house music lovers.

Nest Toronto:
Nest is an underground nightclub in the Little Italy neighborhood, known for its intimate setting and electronic music events. The venue features a Funktion-One sound system and a commitment to showcasing emerging talent in the electronic music scene.

The Drake Underground:
Part of The Drake Hotel complex on Queen Street West, The Drake Underground is a cozy and eclectic nightclub that hosts live music performances, DJ sets, and themed parties. It's a hotspot for those looking for a diverse range of music genres in an intimate setting.

Cabana Pool Bar:

For a unique nightclub experience, Cabana Pool Bar offers a day-to-night party setting. Located on the waterfront, it features poolside cabanas, live DJs, and a vibrant atmosphere. Cabana Pool Bar is a seasonal venue, open during the warmer months.

Toybox Toronto:

Situated in the Entertainment District, Toybox is a stylish and upscale nightclub with a focus on electronic dance music. The venue boasts a visually striking design, LED screens, and a lively dance floor, attracting a fashionable crowd.

EFS Toronto:

EFS (Everything's For Sale) is a nightclub in the King West neighborhood known for its rooftop patio and sleek interior. With a mix of hip-hop, R&B, and electronic beats, EFS offers a sophisticated and high-energy nightlife experience.

CUBE Nightclub:

Located in the heart of the Entertainment District, CUBE is a chic and modern nightclub with a diverse music lineup. It features a mix of live performances,

DJ sets, and themed parties, making it a versatile destination for nightlife enthusiasts.

The Hoxton:
The Hoxton, situated in the King West neighborhood, is a trendy nightclub and live music venue. It showcases a mix of electronic, indie, and alternative music acts, creating an eclectic and lively atmosphere.

These nightclubs represent just a glimpse of Toronto's dynamic nightlife scene. Whether you're into electronic dance music, live performances, or themed parties, the city offers a diverse range of venues to dance the night away.

Live Music Venues

Toronto's vibrant music scene is enriched by a variety of live music venues, catering to different genres and atmospheres. Here's an overview of some notable live music venues in the city:

The Danforth Music Hall:
Originally opened in 1919, The Danforth Music Hall is one of Toronto's oldest and most iconic live music

venues. It hosts a diverse range of performances, including concerts, comedy shows, and special events. The venue's historic charm and excellent acoustics make it a favorite among music enthusiasts.

Massey Hall:
A true Toronto landmark, Massey Hall has been a venue for live music since 1894. Renowned for its excellent sound quality, the hall has hosted legendary performances by artists such as Neil Young, Bob Dylan, and Gordon Lightfoot. After undergoing renovations, Massey Hall continues to be a key player in Toronto's live music scene.

The Horseshoe Tavern:
Established in 1947, The Horseshoe Tavern is a legendary venue in the Queen Street West area. It has played a pivotal role in Toronto's music history, showcasing emerging and established artists. The intimate setting and diverse lineup make it a favorite among both locals and tourists.

Lee's Palace:
Situated in the Annex neighborhood, Lee's Palace is an iconic venue known for its alternative and indie

music scene. With a spacious layout and a balcony overlooking the stage, Lee's Palace has hosted a wide array of bands and artists since its opening in 1985.

Mod Club Theatre:
The Mod Club Theatre, located on College Street, is a popular live music venue that features a mix of concerts, DJ nights, and special events. The venue's intimate setting and modern design create an engaging atmosphere for music lovers.

The Opera House:
Originally a vaudeville theatre dating back to 1909, The Opera House has transformed into a dynamic live music venue. Located in the Riverside neighborhood, it hosts concerts spanning various genres, including rock, indie, and electronic music.

The Phoenix Concert Theatre:
The Phoenix Concert Theatre, situated in the heart of Toronto, is a versatile venue known for its spacious dance floor and mezzanine. It hosts a variety of events, from live music concerts to dance parties, making it a hub for entertainment.

The Velvet Underground:
Located in the Queen Street West area, The Velvet Underground is a popular venue for indie and alternative music. With a focus on emerging artists and a vibrant atmosphere, it contributes to the city's diverse music landscape.

Roy Thomson Hall:
Roy Thomson Hall, nestled in the Entertainment District, is renowned for its classical music performances and events. The venue's exceptional acoustics and elegant design make it a premier destination for orchestral concerts and other musical experiences.

The Rivoli:
The Rivoli, situated in the Queen Street West area, is a multifaceted venue hosting live music, comedy, and other performances. Known for its intimate setting, it has been a launchpad for many successful Canadian artists.

These live music venues showcase Toronto's commitment to offering a diverse range of musical experiences, from historic concert halls to intimate indie clubs.

OUTDOOR ACTIVITIES

Toronto offers a plethora of outdoor activities that allow residents and visitors to embrace the city's natural beauty and recreational spaces. From expansive parks to scenic waterfronts, the options are diverse.

Toronto's extensive network of parks, including High Park and Trinity Bellwoods Park, provides green spaces for picnics, sports, and leisurely strolls. These parks are hubs for community events, outdoor yoga classes, and family-friendly activities.

The Toronto Islands, accessible by ferry, are a beloved escape for those seeking a peaceful retreat with stunning views of the city skyline. Visitors can bike, kayak, or simply enjoy the serene atmosphere on these car-free islands.

The city's waterfront, particularly along the Martin Goodman Trail, offers a scenic route for cyclists, joggers, and walkers. The revitalized waterfront areas feature parks, beaches, and recreational facilities, creating a vibrant outdoor environment.

Highly regarded for its botanical diversity, the Toronto Botanical Garden is a haven for nature enthusiasts. The gardens provide a serene setting for peaceful walks and educational programs about horticulture and sustainable gardening practices.

The Scarborough Bluffs, overlooking Lake Ontario, offer breathtaking cliff-top views and hiking trails. This natural wonder is a popular destination for outdoor enthusiasts seeking a blend of adventure and picturesque landscapes.

For those interested in wildlife, the Toronto Zoo is a vast attraction featuring a wide array of animals in naturalistic habitats. Visitors can explore themed exhibits, attend educational programs, and witness captivating animal shows.

Toronto's extensive system of bike trails, such as the Don Valley Trail and Humber River Trail, provides cyclists with scenic routes through natural landscapes and urban environments. Biking enthusiasts can explore the city's neighborhoods and connect with nature along these well-maintained paths.

During the winter months, Nathan Phillips Square transforms into a lively outdoor space with a skating rink. Skating enthusiasts can enjoy this iconic winter activity against the backdrop of Toronto City Hall.

In summary, Toronto's outdoor activities showcase the city's commitment to providing diverse and accessible spaces for recreation and relaxation. Whether enjoying the greenery of parks, exploring islands, or immersing oneself in nature, Toronto offers a wealth of outdoor experiences for residents and visitors alike.

Parks and Gardens

Toronto is home to an array of parks and gardens that offer residents and visitors a chance to escape the urban hustle and connect with nature. Here's an overview of some notable parks and gardens in the city:

High Park:
High Park, Toronto's largest public park, is a lush oasis spanning 400 acres. Known for its scenic walking trails, sports facilities, and serene Grenadier Pond, High Park is a favorite destination for picnics,

WELCOME TO TORONTO

cherry blossoms in spring, and outdoor activities. The park also houses the High Park Zoo, showcasing a variety of animals.

Trinity Bellwoods Park:
Situated in the trendy Queen Street West neighborhood, Trinity Bellwoods Park is a popular spot for locals. Its expansive green lawns, dog-friendly areas, and community events make it a vibrant hub. The park is surrounded by cafes, shops, and art installations, contributing to its dynamic atmosphere.

Toronto Islands:
Accessible by ferry, the Toronto Islands offer a tranquil escape from the city. With beaches, bike paths, and picnic areas, the islands provide stunning views of the skyline. Centreville Amusement Park on Centre Island adds a family-friendly element to the island experience.

Toronto Botanical Garden:
Nestled in Edwards Gardens, the Toronto Botanical Garden is a haven for plant enthusiasts. Its themed gardens, including the knot garden and the terraced garden, showcase a diverse range of plants. The

gardens offer educational programs, guided tours, and events throughout the year.

Edwards Gardens:
Adjacent to the Toronto Botanical Garden, Edwards Gardens is a beautifully landscaped green space. Visitors can explore its perennial gardens, rockeries, and scenic walking trails. The gardens are particularly stunning in spring when blossoms are in full bloom.

Scarborough Bluffs Park:
Along the eastern shoreline of Toronto, Scarborough Bluffs Park offers awe-inspiring views of towering cliffs overlooking Lake Ontario. Hiking trails lead to viewpoints where visitors can enjoy panoramic vistas. The Bluffers Park Marina adds a nautical touch to this picturesque location.

Riverdale Farm:
Nestled in Cabbagetown, Riverdale Farm provides an authentic rural experience in the heart of the city. This working farm showcases barns, pastures, and farm animals, allowing visitors to escape the urban environment and immerse themselves in a pastoral setting.

Queen's Park:

Located in the downtown core, Queen's Park is not only a green oasis but also home to the Ontario Legislative Building. The park features walking paths, statues, and landscaped areas, making it a peaceful retreat in the midst of the city's political and cultural hub.

Dufferin Grove Park:

Dufferin Grove Park is a community-centric park known for its vibrant atmosphere. With a popular farmers' market, a communal pizza oven, and a natural ice rink in winter, the park fosters a sense of togetherness and engagement.

David A. Balfour Park:

Situated in the Rosedale neighborhood, David A. Balfour Park offers a serene escape with its wooded areas, walking trails, and the Vale of Avoca Ravine. The Beltline Trail passes through this park, providing a scenic route for walkers and cyclists.

In summary, Toronto's parks and gardens provide diverse environments for relaxation, recreation, and appreciation of nature. Whether seeking a peaceful stroll, a family-friendly outing, or a scenic escape, these green spaces contribute to the city's vibrant and livable character.

Hiking and Nature Trails

Toronto and its surrounding areas offer a variety of hiking and nature trails, providing outdoor enthusiasts with opportunities to explore natural landscapes and enjoy the beauty of the region. Here's an overview of some notable hiking and nature trails in and around the city:

Rouge National Urban Park:
Rouge National Urban Park, situated in the eastern part of Toronto, is one of the largest urban parks in North America. It offers a network of trails through diverse ecosystems, including forests, wetlands, and meadows. The Vista Trail provides panoramic views of the Rouge Valley, and the Mast Trail leads to the historic Bead Hill.

Bruce Trail:
The Bruce Trail, stretching over 890 kilometers (550 miles), is one of Canada's longest and most famous hiking trails. While the trail extends beyond

Toronto, the nearby sections offer scenic routes through the Niagara Escarpment, showcasing waterfalls, cliffs, and lush forests. Places like the Elora Gorge and Rattlesnake Point Conservation Area are accessible portions of the Bruce Trail.

Scarborough Bluffs Trail:
The Scarborough Bluffs Trail runs along the eastern edge of Toronto, offering breathtaking views of the towering cliffs and Lake Ontario. The trail allows hikers to explore the Bluffers Park area and witness the natural beauty of the bluffs from various vantage points.

Don Valley Trails:
The Don Valley trails encompass a network of paths along the Don River, providing an urban escape with wooded areas and riverside scenery. Trails like the Crothers Woods Trail and the Lower Don Trail offer a mix of natural landscapes and city views.

Humber Valley Heritage Trail:
The Humber Valley Heritage Trail winds through the Humber River watershed, offering a mix of natural terrain and cultural points of interest. The trail spans over 30 kilometers, passing through

forests, meadows, and along the banks of the Humber River.

Toronto Islands Trails:
The Toronto Islands are not only a scenic getaway but also feature a network of walking and cycling trails. Trails on Centre Island and Ward's Island allow visitors to explore beaches, parks, and natural areas while enjoying stunning views of the city skyline.

E.T. Seton Park Trail:
E.T. Seton Park, located in the Don River watershed, offers a network of trails through wooded areas and along the West Don River. The park is known for its naturalized landscapes, making it a peaceful retreat within the city.

Tommy Thompson Park (Leslie Street Spit):
Tommy Thompson Park, also known as the Leslie Street Spit, is a man-made peninsula that has become a haven for wildlife. The park features trails that offer views of Lake Ontario and downtown Toronto, with opportunities for birdwatching and enjoying natural habitats.

Evergreen Brick Works Trails:
The Evergreen Brick Works site has several trails that wind through its revitalized industrial landscape and the adjacent Don Valley. The trails provide opportunities to explore the Don River, wetlands, and the picturesque Quarry Garden.

Glen Stewart Ravine:
Glen Stewart Ravine is a hidden gem in the Beaches neighborhood, offering a secluded trail through a lush ravine. The trail follows a meandering creek, providing a serene escape from the urban surroundings.

In summary, Toronto and its surrounding areas provide a diverse range of hiking and nature trails, allowing outdoor enthusiasts to discover scenic landscapes, experience nature, and enjoy recreational activities throughout the year.

Waterfront Activities

Toronto's waterfront is a bustling and scenic area that offers a wide range of activities for residents and visitors alike. Here's an overview of some notable waterfront activities in the city:

Harbourfront Centre:

Harbourfront Centre is a cultural and recreational hub located along the shores of Lake Ontario. It hosts a variety of events and activities, including outdoor concerts, art installations, and festivals. The boardwalk area is perfect for leisurely strolls with stunning views of the lake.

Toronto Islands:

Accessible by ferry, the Toronto Islands are a popular destination for a variety of waterfront activities. Visitors can enjoy picnics, bike rentals, and beaches on the islands. Centre Island, Ward's Island, and Hanlan's Point offer different atmospheres, from family-friendly areas to clothing-optional beaches.

Ontario Place:

Ontario Place, situated on the waterfront, features a mix of entertainment options. The park offers outdoor concerts, festivals, and events during the warmer months. The iconic Cinesphere and the pods, which host immersive exhibits, add to the waterfront experience.

Sugar Beach:
Sugar Beach is a vibrant urban beach located near the Redpath Sugar Refinery. The pink umbrellas and sandy shores create a picturesque setting for relaxation. It's a great spot for sunbathing, picnics, and enjoying the waterfront atmosphere.

Martin Goodman Trail:
The Martin Goodman Trail runs along the waterfront, providing a scenic route for cyclists, joggers, and walkers. The trail stretches from the Humber Bay Arch Bridge in the west

Seasonal Activities (Winter sports, summer festivals)

Toronto offers a diverse array of seasonal activities throughout the year, embracing the unique characteristics of each season. Here's an overview of some notable seasonal activities in the city:

Winter:

1. Winter Sports at Nathan Phillips Square:
   - Nathan Phillips Square transforms into a winter wonderland with a large outdoor skating rink.

Skaters can glide under the iconic Toronto sign and the illuminated city skyline.

2. Toronto Christmas Market:

- The Distillery District hosts the Toronto Christmas Market, a festive celebration featuring holiday-themed decorations, local vendors, and seasonal treats. It's a charming destination for shopping and spreading holiday cheer.

3. Winter Festivals and Events:

- Various winter festivals take place, such as the Cavalcade of Lights, which marks the official start of the holiday season with a tree lighting ceremony, fireworks, and live performances.

4. Skiing and Snowboarding:

- While Toronto itself may not have ski resorts, there are nearby destinations like Blue Mountain and Horseshoe Resort where winter sports enthusiasts can enjoy skiing, snowboarding, and other snow-related activities.

5. Winterlicious:

- Winterlicious is an annual culinary event where participating restaurants across the city offer prix-fixe menus, allowing residents and visitors to explore Toronto's diverse culinary scene.

Spring:

1. Cherry Blossoms in High Park:
   - High Park becomes a floral paradise in spring when cherry blossoms bloom. The Sakura trees attract crowds eager to witness the beauty of these delicate pink flowers.

2. Toronto Flower Market:
   - The Toronto Flower Market, held in various locations, celebrates the arrival of spring with a vibrant showcase of locally grown flowers. It's a great place to purchase fresh blooms and gardening supplies.

3. Doors Open Toronto:
   - Doors Open Toronto provides the opportunity to explore the city's architecture and heritage as numerous buildings, including historical landmarks and modern structures, open their doors to the public.

4. Spring Festivals:

- Spring brings various festivals, such as the Toronto International Film Festival (TIFF) Kids International Film Festival, featuring family-friendly films and activities.

Summer:

1. Toronto International Film Festival (TIFF):
- TIFF is a major cultural event that takes place in September, showcasing a diverse selection of international and Canadian films. It attracts filmmakers, celebrities, and film enthusiasts from around the world.

2. Beaches Jazz Festival:
- The Beaches Jazz Festival is a lively summer event featuring a series of concerts, street performances, and a vibrant parade along Queen Street East.

3. Toronto Caribbean Carnival (Caribana):
- Caribana is North America's largest Caribbean carnival, celebrating Caribbean culture with vibrant parades, live music, and cultural events throughout the city.

4. Toronto Islands and Beaches:

- Summer is the perfect time to enjoy the Toronto Islands and the city's beaches, including Woodbine Beach and Sugar Beach. Activities include picnics, beach volleyball, kayaking, and paddleboarding.

5. Outdoor Concerts and Music Festivals:

- Various outdoor concerts and music festivals take place in parks and venues across the city, featuring a wide range of musical genres.

Fall:

1. Toronto International Film Festival (TIFF):

- TIFF continues into the fall, showcasing a selection of acclaimed films and attracting filmmakers, industry professionals, and film enthusiasts.

2. Nuit Blanche:

- Nuit Blanche is an all-night contemporary art event that transforms the city with installations, performances, and interactive art projects, attracting art lovers and creatives.

3. Fall Foliage in High Park:

Page|169

- High Park's lush greenery transforms into a spectrum of autumn colors, making it a popular destination for fall foliage walks and photography.

4. Thanksgiving Parade:
- Toronto's Thanksgiving Parade is a family-friendly event featuring giant balloons, floats, and marching bands, creating a festive atmosphere in celebration of Thanksgiving.

These seasonal activities contribute to Toronto's dynamic and ever-changing cultural landscape, offering something special for residents and visitors to enjoy throughout the year.

WELCOME TO TORONTO

DAY TRIPS FROM TORONTO

Toronto's strategic location in southern Ontario provides easy access to a variety of day trip destinations, ranging from natural wonders to charming towns. Here's an overview of some popular day trip options from Toronto:

Niagara Falls:
A classic day trip destination, Niagara Falls is just a 1.5 to 2-hour drive from Toronto. Witness the awe-inspiring beauty of the falls, take a boat tour like Maid of the Mist to get up close, explore the nearby town of Niagara-on-the-Lake with its wineries and historic charm, or visit attractions like the Niagara Parks Butterfly Conservatory.

Prince Edward County:
Known for its wineries, picturesque landscapes, and charming small towns, Prince Edward County is approximately a 2.5-hour drive from Toronto. Enjoy wine tasting at local vineyards, explore the artistic community in Wellington, and relax on the beaches of Sandbanks Provincial Park.

Royal Botanical Gardens and Dundurn Castle in Hamilton:
Hamilton, just an hour's drive from Toronto, offers the Royal Botanical Gardens with its diverse plant collections and beautiful landscapes. Nearby, Dundurn Castle provides a glimpse into Canadian history with its 40-room mansion and lush grounds.

St. Jacobs and Elora Gorge:
St. Jacobs, known for its Mennonite heritage, is around a 1.5-hour drive from Toronto. Explore the St. Jacobs Farmers' Market, stroll through the village, and enjoy the picturesque countryside. On the way back, consider a stop at Elora Gorge, where you can hike and appreciate the stunning landscapes.

Stratford:
Famous for its annual Stratford Festival, this charming town is approximately a 2-hour drive from Toronto. Enjoy a day of theatrical performances, explore the town's architecture, and dine at one of its many fine restaurants.

Toronto Islands:

Although technically part of Toronto, a day trip to the Toronto Islands offers a unique escape from the city's hustle and bustle. Take a ferry from downtown Toronto to the islands and enjoy the beaches, bike trails, and stunning views of the skyline.

Rattlesnake Point Conservation Area:
Located within an hour's drive from Toronto, Rattlesnake Point offers hiking trails with panoramic views of the Niagara Escarpment. The area is popular for rock climbing and provides a peaceful natural retreat.

Blue Mountain Village:
Around a 2-hour drive from Toronto, Blue Mountain Village is a year-round destination. In the winter, it's known for skiing and snowboarding, while the warmer months offer hiking, mountain biking, and a vibrant pedestrian village with shops and restaurants.

Toronto Zoo and Scarborough Bluffs:
Combine a visit to the Toronto Zoo with a scenic drive to the nearby Scarborough Bluffs. The bluffs provide breathtaking views of Lake Ontario and are a great spot for hiking and photography.

Canada's Wonderland:
For thrill-seekers, Canada's Wonderland amusement park is a short drive from Toronto. Spend a day riding roller coasters, enjoying water rides, and exploring the entertainment complex.

These day trip options cater to a variety of interests, from nature lovers and history enthusiasts to those seeking adventure or cultural experiences. Whether exploring the natural wonders surrounding Toronto or immersing oneself in the local history and arts of nearby towns, there's a diverse range of day trip destinations to choose from.

Niagara Falls

Certainly! Here's a guide to a day trip to Niagara Falls from Toronto in a more structured format, including suggested times:

Morning:
1. 7:00 AM - Departure:
   - Start your day early to beat the traffic. Leave Toronto around 7:00 AM to ensure a full day of exploration.

2. 8:30 AM - Breakfast En Route:

- Grab breakfast on the way. There are several cafes and breakfast spots along the route.

Late Morning:
3. 10:00 AM - Arrival at Niagara Falls:

- Arrive at Niagara Falls by 10:00 AM. Park at one of the designated parking areas.

4. 10:30 AM - Explore Niagara Falls:

- Head to the iconic Horseshoe Falls. Take a stroll along the Niagara Parkway to enjoy different viewpoints. Consider visiting Table Rock Welcome Centre for an overview.

Early Afternoon:
5. 12:00 PM - Lunch:

- Enjoy lunch with a view. There are various restaurants overlooking the falls, or you can opt for a picnic in Queen Victoria Park.

6. 1:30 PM - Maid of the Mist Boat Tour:

- Experience the power of the falls up close with the Maid of the Mist boat tour. This iconic experience takes you into the mist of the Horseshoe Falls.

Afternoon:
7. 3:00 PM - Explore Clifton Hill:
   - Head to Clifton Hill, known as the "Street of Fun." Explore the entertainment district with its attractions, souvenir shops, and themed restaurants.

8. 4:30 PM - Journey Behind the Falls:
   - Visit Journey Behind the Falls for a unique perspective. This attraction takes you behind the falls through tunnels for an immersive experience.

Evening:
9. 6:00 PM - Dinner:
   - Enjoy dinner in the Niagara Falls area. Many restaurants offer both casual and fine dining options.

10. 8:00 PM - Illumination of the Falls:
   - Don't miss the nightly illumination of the falls. The falls are beautifully lit with colorful lights, creating a mesmerizing spectacle.

Late Evening:
11. 9:00 PM - Departure to Toronto:

- Head back to Toronto around 9:00 PM. This allows you to avoid the rush and enjoy a more relaxed drive back.

12. 10:30 PM - Return to Toronto:
- Arrive back in Toronto around 10:30 PM, concluding your day trip to Niagara Falls.

This itinerary is flexible, and you can adjust the times based on your preferences. Additionally, it's advisable to check the opening hours and availability of attractions in advance.

Wine Country

A day trip to Ontario's wine country from Toronto is a delightful experience, offering a chance to explore vineyards, taste local wines, and enjoy the picturesque landscapes. Here's a guide to a day trip to wine country:

Morning:
1. 8:00 AM - Departure from Toronto:
- Start your day early to make the most of your wine country adventure. Depart from Toronto around 8:00 AM.

2. 10:00 AM - Arrive in Niagara-on-the-Lake:
- Head to Niagara-on-the-Lake, the heart of Ontario's wine region. This charming town is not only known for its wineries but also for its historic architecture and quaint streets.

Late Morning:
3. 11:00 AM - First Winery Visit:
- Begin your wine tasting journey with a visit to a local winery. Many wineries open around 11:00 AM. Consider iconic ones like Peller Estates, Inniskillin, or Trius Winery.

4. 12:30 PM - Lunch:
- Enjoy a leisurely lunch at a winery or a local restaurant. Some wineries have on-site restaurants offering farm-to-table cuisine paired with their wines.

Afternoon:
5. 2:00 PM - Explore More Wineries:
- Visit additional wineries in the region. Explore both large estates and boutique wineries to experience the diversity of Ontario's wine offerings.

6. 4:00 PM - Wine Tours and Experiences:

- Participate in guided tours or unique wine experiences offered by some wineries. This could include vineyard tours, cellar tastings, or even blending your own wine.

Early Evening:
7. 6:00 PM - Dinner:

- Have dinner at a winery or a local restaurant. Many wineries offer dining options with scenic views of the vineyards.

8. 8:00 PM - Sunset Stroll:

- Take a stroll through Niagara-on-the-Lake as the sun sets. The town has a serene ambiance, especially in the evening.

Late Evening:
9. 9:00 PM - Departure to Toronto:

- Begin your journey back to Toronto around 9:00 PM. Consider taking a scenic route to enjoy nighttime views.

10. 11:00 PM - Return to Toronto:

- Arrive back in Toronto around 11:00 PM, concluding your day trip to wine country.

Tips:
- Designated Driver or Tour: If you plan on wine tasting, consider having a designated driver or joining a guided wine tour to ensure a safe return to Toronto.

- Wine Country Events: Check for any special events or festivals happening in wine country, as they can add a unique touch to your day trip.

- Wine Purchases: If you find wines you love, many wineries allow you to purchase bottles directly. Be sure to inquire about shipping options if needed.

- Reservations: Some wineries, especially for tours and experiences, may require reservations. Check in advance and plan accordingly.

This itinerary provides a balance of wine tasting, culinary experiences, and the charm of Niagara-on-the-Lake. Adjustments can be made based on personal preferences and the time of year.

Hamilton – The Waterfall Capital

A day trip to Hamilton, often referred to as "The Waterfall Capital of the World," promises a blend of natural beauty, outdoor adventures, and cultural exploration. Here's a guide to exploring Hamilton and its renowned waterfalls:

Morning:
1. 8:00 AM - Departure from Toronto:
- Begin your journey from Toronto to Hamilton around 8:00 AM. The drive takes approximately one hour, allowing for an early start to your day.

2. 9:00 AM - Arrival in Hamilton:
- Arrive in Hamilton and start your day with a visit to a local café or bakery for a delightful breakfast.

Late Morning:
3. 10:00 AM - Dundurn Castle:
- Explore Dundurn Castle, a National Historic Site, showcasing 40 rooms in a magnificent 19th-century mansion. Learn about the history of the city and its role in Canadian heritage.

4. 11:30 AM - Hamilton Art Gallery:

- Visit the Art Gallery of Hamilton to appreciate a diverse collection of Canadian and international art. The gallery often features exhibitions, ensuring a dynamic experience.

Afternoon:
5. 1:00 PM - Lunch at Augusta Street:
- Head to Augusta Street for lunch, known for its vibrant atmosphere and diverse culinary options. Enjoy a meal at one of the local eateries.

6. 2:30 PM - Waterfall Hike - Webster's Falls and Tew Falls:
- Embark on a scenic hike to Webster's Falls and Tew Falls in the Spencer Gorge Conservation Area. These stunning waterfalls are among Hamilton's most famous and offer picturesque views.

Early Evening:
7. 5:00 PM - Explore Westdale Village:
- Visit Westdale Village, a charming neighborhood near McMaster University. Explore the local shops, cafes, and enjoy a leisurely stroll.

8. 6:30 PM - Dinner in Locke Street:

- Head to Locke Street for dinner, where you'll find a variety of restaurants serving diverse cuisines. Locke Street South is known for its welcoming community and culinary offerings.

Nighttime:
9. 8:00 PM - Hamilton Waterfront:
- Conclude your day with a visit to the Hamilton waterfront. Enjoy a peaceful evening stroll, taking in the views of the harbor and city lights.

10. 9:00 PM - Departure to Toronto:
- Begin your journey back to Toronto around 9:00 PM, allowing you to return comfortably.

11. 10:00 PM - Return to Toronto:
- Arrive back in Toronto around 10:00 PM, concluding your day trip to Hamilton.

Tips:
- Waterfall Safety: If you plan to explore waterfalls, wear appropriate footwear and exercise caution on trails, especially if they are wet or uneven.

- Check Event Calendar: Hamilton often hosts events, festivals, and markets. Check the city's event calendar to see if there's anything special happening during your visit.

- Scenic Drives: Consider taking scenic drives around Hamilton to enjoy the natural landscapes and views of the city.

This itinerary provides a mix of cultural exploration, outdoor activities, and culinary experiences, allowing you to make the most of your day trip to Hamilton.

Toronto Islands

A day trip to the Toronto Islands offers a peaceful escape from the bustling city, providing a combination of outdoor activities, scenic views, and a relaxed island atmosphere. Here's a guide to exploring the Toronto Islands:

Morning:
1. 8:00 AM - Departure from Toronto:
   - Catch the ferry from the Jack Layton Ferry Terminal at the foot of Bay Street. Ferries operate regularly, and the journey takes about 15 minutes.

2. 8:30 AM - Arrival on Toronto Islands:
- Arrive on Centre Island and start your day early to make the most of your time. Begin with a visit to Centreville Amusement Park if you're traveling with family.

Late Morning:
3. 10:00 AM - Bicycle Rentals:
- Rent bicycles at one of the rental shops on Centre Island. Cycling is a popular way to explore the islands, offering flexibility and the chance to cover more ground.

4. 11:00 AM - Explore Ward's Island:
- Cycle or walk to Ward's Island. Enjoy the serene residential atmosphere, stroll along the sandy beaches, and take in the picturesque views of Lake Ontario.

Afternoon:
5. 12:30 PM - Picnic Lunch at Hanlan's Point:
- Head to Hanlan's Point and find a scenic spot for a picnic. Hanlan's Point Beach is known for its tranquility and offers a great place to relax and enjoy your meal.

6. 2:00 PM - Beach Time and Water Activities:
- Spend the afternoon on one of the beaches, either at Hanlan's Point or Centre Island Beach. Take a dip in the lake or try paddleboarding and kayaking, available for rent.

Early Evening:
7. 4:30 PM - Explore Gibraltar Point Lighthouse:
- Visit the historic Gibraltar Point Lighthouse. It's a peaceful spot with a scenic backdrop, providing a glimpse into the island's history.

8. 6:00 PM - Dinner at Toronto Island BBQ & Beer Co.:
- Enjoy dinner at Toronto Island BBQ & Beer Co. near Centre Island. This laid-back eatery offers barbecue delights and a relaxing atmosphere.

Nighttime:
9. 8:00 PM - Sunset at Centre Island:
- Head back to Centre Island to catch the sunset. The Toronto skyline provides a stunning backdrop as the sun dips below the horizon.

10. 9:00 PM - Evening Ferry Ride:

- Take the ferry back to the mainland. The city lights and skyline views during the evening ferry ride add to the enchanting experience.

11. 10:00 PM - Return to Toronto:
    - Arrive back in Toronto around 10:00 PM, concluding your day trip to the Toronto Islands.

Tips:
- Ferry Schedule: Check the ferry schedule in advance, as the frequency may vary based on the season and day of the week.

- Island Events: Keep an eye out for special events or festivals happening on the islands. They can add an extra layer of enjoyment to your visit.

- Weather Considerations: Be mindful of weather conditions, especially if you plan to engage in water activities. Dress accordingly and stay updated on any weather advisories.

This itinerary is designed to capture the natural beauty and recreational opportunities the Toronto Islands offer, providing a perfect day of relaxation and exploration. Adjustments can be made based on personal preferences and the time of year.

PRACTICAL INFORMATION

Navigating Toronto:
Toronto boasts an extensive public transportation system operated by the Toronto Transit Commission (TTC), including buses, subways, and streetcars. Taxis and ride-sharing services like Uber provide additional transportation options.

Weather:
Toronto experiences four distinct seasons. Winters can be cold with snow, while summers are warm and humid. Visitors should check the weather forecast and dress accordingly.

Currency:
The official currency is the Canadian Dollar (CAD), and credit/debit cards are widely accepted. ATMs are prevalent for currency withdrawal.

Language:
English is the primary language in Toronto, but due to its multicultural nature, residents often speak multiple languages.

Electricity:

Toronto operates on a 120-volt electrical system with Type A and Type B outlets. Travelers may need adapters or transformers based on their home country's voltage and plug types.

Safety:
Toronto is generally considered safe. Travelers should exercise standard safety precautions, such as staying aware of surroundings and securing belongings.

Health and Emergency Services:
Toronto offers a well-equipped healthcare system, with hospitals, clinics, and pharmacies. Emergency services can be accessed by dialing 911.

Time Zone:
Toronto operates on Eastern Standard Time (EST) during the non-daylight saving period and Eastern Daylight Time (EDT) during daylight saving time.

Tourist Information Centers:
Tourism Toronto operates information centers throughout the city, providing maps, brochures, and assistance for travelers.

Internet and Connectivity:
Wi-Fi is widely available in hotels, cafes, and public spaces. Visitors can purchase SIM cards for mobile data if reliable connectivity is needed.

Cultural Etiquette:
Toronto's diversity is reflected in its cultural etiquette. Respect for cultural differences is appreciated, and polite greetings are customary. Tipping is standard in restaurants, typically ranging from 15% to 20%.

Customs and Entry Requirements:
Visitors should check entry requirements before travel. Depending on nationality, a visa, Electronic Travel Authorization (eTA), or other documentation may be required.

These practical details aim to enhance the overall travel experience by providing essential information for navigating the city, ensuring safety, and respecting local customs and regulations.

Weather and Best Time to Visit

Toronto experiences four distinct seasons, each offering a different atmosphere and range of activities. Understanding the weather can help visitors plan their trips accordingly.

Spring (March to May):
- Spring in Toronto brings milder temperatures, blossoming flowers, and the awakening of greenery in parks. Daytime temperatures range from 5°C to 20°C (41°F to 68°F). It's an ideal time for exploring outdoor attractions and enjoying spring festivals.

Summer (June to August):
- Summer is the peak tourist season in Toronto. The city comes alive with warm temperatures ranging from 20°C to 30°C (68°F to 86°F). This season offers ideal conditions for outdoor activities, festivals, and exploring the Toronto Islands or waterfront.

Fall (September to November):
- Fall in Toronto features cooler temperatures and vibrant autumn foliage, particularly in parks like High Park. Daytime temperatures range from 10°C

to 20°C (50°F to 68°F). It's a great time for scenic walks, fall festivals, and enjoying the changing colors.

Winter (December to February):
- Winter brings cold temperatures and snowfall to Toronto. Daytime temperatures range from -1°C to 5°C (30°F to 41°F), with occasional colder days. Winter enthusiasts can enjoy outdoor activities like ice skating at Nathan Phillips Square or skiing near the city.

Best Time to Visit:
- The best time to visit Toronto depends on personal preferences and desired activities. Summer (June to August) is popular for outdoor events, festivals, and pleasant weather. Spring and fall offer milder temperatures and scenic beauty, making them favorable for outdoor exploration. Winter is suitable for those who enjoy winter sports or the festive holiday season.

Considerations:
- Peak Tourist Season: Summer is the busiest season with peak tourist activity. Accommodations and

attractions may be crowded, but the warm weather allows for extensive outdoor exploration.

- Shoulder Seasons: Spring and fall are considered shoulder seasons, offering a balance between favorable weather and fewer crowds. This is a good time for a more relaxed visit.

- Winter Activities: Winter enthusiasts can enjoy the festive atmosphere, winter sports, and cultural events. However, some outdoor attractions may have limited accessibility during colder months.

- Festivals and Events: Check the city's event calendar for festivals, events, and special activities that may align with your travel dates.

Understanding Toronto's weather patterns and seasonal highlights can help visitors plan a trip that aligns with their preferences and desired experiences.

Currency and Money Matters

Currency:

- The official currency of Toronto is the Canadian Dollar (CAD).

Currency Exchange:
- Currency exchange services are widely available at banks, currency exchange offices, and airports. Automated teller machines (ATMs) are also common and accept international debit and credit cards.

Credit Cards:
- Credit and debit cards are widely accepted in Toronto. Visa and MasterCard are the most commonly used, followed by American Express and Discover. It's advisable to inform your bank about your travel plans to avoid any issues with card usage.

ATMs:
- ATMs are prevalent throughout the city, providing easy access to cash. They are commonly found at banks, shopping centers, and major tourist areas. Most ATMs accept major international debit and credit cards.

Tipping:

- Tipping is customary in Toronto. In restaurants, a standard tip is around 15% to 20% of the bill. It's common to tip taxi drivers, hotel staff, and other service providers as well.

Shopping:
- Major credit cards are widely accepted in shops and malls. When using a credit card for purchases, be aware that some establishments may ask for photo identification.

Budgeting:
- Toronto can be considered moderately expensive. Prices for accommodation, dining, and attractions vary. It's advisable to have a mix of cash and cards for convenience.

Sales Tax:
- The Harmonized Sales Tax (HST) applies to most goods and services in Toronto. The HST is a combined federal and provincial tax, and the current rate is 13%. Prices displayed in stores generally do not include tax, so the final amount will be higher at the checkout.

Bargaining:

- Bargaining is not a common practice in Toronto, especially in retail stores and restaurants. Prices are generally fixed, and discounts are usually offered during sales or promotional periods.

Safety Tips:
- Keep an eye on your belongings, especially in crowded areas, to prevent theft.
- Notify your bank of your travel dates to avoid any issues with card transactions.
- Use reputable currency exchange services to ensure fair rates.

Understanding the local currency, payment options, and tipping practices will contribute to a smooth and enjoyable experience when it comes to managing money matters in Toronto.

Safety Tips

1. General Awareness:
- Stay aware of your surroundings, especially in crowded areas, public transportation, and tourist hotspots.
- Keep valuables secure and avoid displaying expensive items openly.

2. Public Transportation:

- Use official and well-marked transportation services. The Toronto Transit Commission (TTC) is a safe and reliable option for getting around the city.

- Be cautious of pickpockets in crowded areas, such as subway stations and buses.

3. Neighbourhood Safety:

- Toronto is generally a safe city, but like any major urban area, it has neighbourhoods with varying levels of safety. Research neighbourhoods before visiting and be cautious in unfamiliar areas, especially at night.

4. Emergency Services:

- Familiarize yourself with emergency contact numbers. In Canada, the emergency number is 911 for police, fire, and medical emergencies.

5. Weather Preparedness:

- Be prepared for changing weather conditions, especially during winter. Dress appropriately and check the weather forecast before heading out.

6. Water Safety:

- If visiting the Toronto Islands or other waterfront areas, adhere to safety guidelines and be cautious around bodies of water, especially if with children.

7. Health and Medical Care:
- Toronto has a well-developed healthcare system. In case of medical emergencies, dial 911.
- Ensure you have travel insurance that covers healthcare expenses during your stay.

8. Transportation Safety:
- When using taxis or ride-sharing services, ensure they are legitimate and marked. Always check the driver's identification.
- Follow traffic rules and pedestrian signals when crossing streets.

9. Cybersecurity:
- Use secure Wi-Fi connections, especially when accessing personal or financial information.
- Be cautious about sharing personal information online and avoid public computers for sensitive transactions.

10. Cultural Sensitivity:

- Respect cultural diversity. Toronto is a multicultural city, and being open-minded enhances the travel experience.

11. COVID-19 Precautions:
- Stay informed about current COVID-19 guidelines and follow recommended health and safety measures.
- Adhere to public health protocols, such as wearing masks in indoor spaces if required.

12. Wildlife Awareness:
- If exploring natural areas, be aware of local wildlife and follow guidelines to avoid encounters or conflicts.

13. Local Laws and Regulations:
- Familiarize yourself with local laws and regulations. Different areas may have specific rules regarding activities like smoking, alcohol consumption, or recreational use of certain substances.

14. Emergency Contacts:

- Keep a list of important contacts, including the local embassy or consulate, your accommodation, and local emergency services.

By staying vigilant, informed, and following these safety tips, visitors can enjoy a secure and memorable experience in Toronto. Always prioritize personal safety and take necessary precautions to ensure a positive travel experience.

Local Etiquette

1. Politeness and Friendliness:
- Canadians, including Torontonians, are known for their politeness and friendliness. Greet people with a smile and use polite language in interactions.

2. Queuing:
- Canadians typically adhere to queues or lines in a respectful manner. Wait your turn in various situations, such as public transportation, elevators, or when entering buildings.

3. Apologies and Excuses:
- Canadians are known for saying "sorry" and "excuse me" frequently. It's a cultural norm to

apologize for minor inconveniences or even when someone else bumps into you.

4. Tipping Culture:

- Tipping is customary in Toronto, particularly in restaurants, cafes, and for services like taxi rides. A standard tip is around 15% to 20% of the total bill.

5. Punctuality:

- Being punctual is valued in Toronto. Arrive on time for appointments, meetings, and social gatherings.

6. Multicultural Respect:

- Toronto is one of the most multicultural cities globally, and residents appreciate diversity. Be respectful of different cultures, customs, and languages.

7. Public Transportation Etiquette:

- When using public transportation, wait for passengers to exit before boarding.
- Offer your seat to those who may need it, such as seniors, pregnant women, or individuals with disabilities.

8. Dining Etiquette:

- When dining out, wait for everyone to be served before starting your meal.

- Keep your elbows off the table, and use cutlery appropriately.

9. Dress Code:

- Toronto is a diverse and accepting city, allowing for a range of styles. However, dress appropriately for specific venues or events.

10. Environmental Consciousness:

- Toronto places importance on sustainability and environmental consciousness. Dispose of trash properly, recycle, and be mindful of your ecological impact.

11. Handshakes and Personal Space:

- Handshakes are a common greeting. Maintain a comfortable amount of personal space during interactions.

12. Quiet Public Spaces:

- Maintain a lower volume of conversation in public spaces, such as libraries, museums, and public transportation.

13. Gift-Giving:
- If invited to someone's home, it's customary to bring a small gift, such as flowers or chocolates, as a token of appreciation.

14. Respect for Indigenous Culture:
- Acknowledge and respect the Indigenous heritage and culture. Learn about the traditional territories and histories of the local Indigenous peoples.

15. Acceptance of LGBT+ Community:
- Toronto is known for its acceptance of the LGBT+ community. Respect diversity in sexual orientation and gender identity.

By embracing these local etiquette practices, visitors can contribute to a positive and respectful atmosphere in Toronto, fostering meaningful interactions with locals and enhancing their overall experience in the city.

USEFUL RESOURCES

Toronto provides a range of resources to assist visitors in navigating the city and enhancing their experience:

1. Tourism Toronto:

- Tourism Toronto is the official destination marketing organization for the city. Their website, visitor centers, and information booths provide maps, brochures, and details about attractions and events.

2. Visitor Information Centers:

- Located at key points throughout the city, visitor information centers offer assistance and resources for tourists. These centers provide helpful staff, brochures, and information about current events.

3. City Maps and Apps:

- Toronto offers detailed city maps at visitor information centers, hotels, and transportation hubs. Additionally, mobile apps such as Google Maps and transit apps help with navigation and finding local attractions.

4. Toronto Public Library:

- The Toronto Public Library is not only a great resource for literature but also for information about the city. Visitors can access maps, guides, and attend local events held at library branches.

5. Transportation Information:

- The Toronto Transit Commission (TTC) website and customer service provide information on public transportation routes, schedules, and fare details. Transportation hubs and stations also offer assistance.

6. Event Listings:

- Online platforms like BlogTO, Now Magazine, and Toronto.com provide comprehensive event listings, including festivals, concerts, and cultural happenings.

7. Emergency Services:

- Familiarize yourself with emergency services by saving important numbers, such as 911 for emergencies and local police contacts.

8. Wi-Fi Hotspots:

- Toronto offers free Wi-Fi in various public spaces, including parks, libraries, and some downtown areas. Check for Wi-Fi availability to stay connected.

9. Weather Updates:
- Stay informed about the weather through reliable weather websites, apps, or local news channels to plan activities accordingly.

10. Currency Exchange:
- Locate currency exchange offices or banks to exchange money. Airport kiosks and downtown locations are common places for currency exchange.

11. Consulates and Embassies:
- Know the location and contact details of your country's consulate or embassy in case of emergencies or assistance.

12. Local News Outlets:
- Stay informed about local news, events, and any advisories through Toronto's local news outlets, radio stations, or news websites.

13. Medical Services:

- Identify nearby hospitals, clinics, and pharmacies. In case of medical emergencies, dial 911 or visit the nearest medical facility.

14. Online Forums and Communities:
- Engage with online forums and travel communities where locals and experienced travelers share insights, tips, and recommendations about Toronto.

Accessing these resources will help visitors make the most of their time in Toronto, stay informed, and navigate the city with ease. Whether seeking event information, transportation details, or emergency assistance, these resources contribute to a seamless travel experience.

Tourist Information Centers

Tourist Information Centers are valuable resources for visitors, providing assistance, maps, and information about attractions. Here are some notable Tourist Information Centers in Toronto:

1. Tourism Toronto Visitor Centre:

- Located in the heart of downtown Toronto, this center is operated by Tourism Toronto and offers a wealth of information, including brochures, maps, and expert advice on local attractions and events.

2. Union Station Visitor Information Centre:

- Situated within Union Station, one of the city's major transportation hubs, this center provides convenient access for arriving visitors. It offers assistance with travel planning and maps.

3. Toronto Pearson International Airport Visitor Information:

- The airport's information desks are equipped to assist travelers with city information, transportation options, and general inquiries. They are strategically placed in the arrivals area.

4. Casa Loma Visitor Services:

- At Casa Loma, a historic castle and popular attraction, visitor services include information about the castle's history, guided tours, and details about nearby points of interest.

5. Harbourfront Centre Information Desk:

- Located in the Harbourfront Centre, this information desk caters to tourists exploring the waterfront area. It provides details on cultural events, performances, and nearby attractions.

6. Toronto Islands Information Booth:
- On Centre Island, there is an information booth providing details about ferry schedules, island attractions, and assistance for visitors exploring the Toronto Islands.

7. Royal Ontario Museum Visitor Services:
- The Royal Ontario Museum (ROM) offers visitor services that include information about exhibits, guided tours, and additional insights into the museum's collections.

8. Art Gallery of Ontario (AGO) Information Desk:
- At the AGO, visitors can find an information desk offering details about current exhibitions, guided tours, and special events happening at the gallery.

9. City Hall Visitor Services:

- Toronto City Hall has an information desk that provides details about the building's architecture, city services, and nearby attractions, including Nathan Phillips Square.

10. Eaton Centre Guest Services:

- Located within the Toronto Eaton Centre, one of the city's premier shopping destinations, this service desk assists visitors with mall information, store locations, and city maps.

11. St. Lawrence Market Information Desk:

- At the St. Lawrence Market, a historic marketplace, the information desk provides details about market vendors, special events, and nearby culinary attractions.

These Tourist Information Centers are strategically placed across Toronto, ensuring that visitors have easy access to assistance and information as they explore the city and its diverse attractions.

Emergency Contacts

In case of emergencies or urgent assistance, it's important to be aware of the following contact information in Toronto:

1. Emergency Services:

- Dial 911 for immediate assistance in case of fire, police, medical emergencies, or any situation requiring urgent attention.

2. Non-Emergency Police Services:

- For non-emergency situations that still require police assistance, you can contact the Toronto Police Service at 416-808-2222.

3. Ambulance and Medical Emergencies:

- For medical emergencies requiring an ambulance, dial 911. Emergency Medical Services (EMS) will respond promptly.

4. Fire Department:

- In case of a fire or related emergency, dial 911. The Toronto Fire Services will respond to the situation.

5. Poison Control:

- If you suspect poisoning or require information about potential hazards, contact the Ontario Poison Centre at 1-800-268-9017.

6. Toronto Transit Commission (TTC) Safety Concerns:

- To report safety concerns or emergencies related to TTC services, call 416-393-3030.

7. Consulates and Embassies:

- Contact your country's consulate or embassy in Toronto for assistance related to travel documentation or other consular services.

8. Toronto Public Health:

- For health-related inquiries or to report public health concerns, contact Toronto Public Health at 416-338-7600.

9. Victim Services Toronto:

- If you are a victim of crime and require support, contact Victim Services Toronto at 416-808-7066.

10. Roadside Assistance:

- If you experience car trouble or require roadside assistance, contact a local towing service or your automobile association.

11. Toronto Hydro (Power Outages):
- For power outages or electrical emergencies, contact Toronto Hydro at 416-542-8000.

12. Toronto Water (Water Emergencies):
- If you experience water-related emergencies or issues, contact Toronto Water at 416-392-2489.

13. Toronto Animal Services:
- For animal-related emergencies or concerns, contact Toronto Animal Services at 416-338-7297.

14. Mental Health Support:
- If you or someone you know is in crisis and requires mental health support, contact the Gerstein Centre Crisis Line at 416-929-5200.

It's advisable to save these emergency contacts in your phone or keep them in a readily accessible location. In any emergency, always dial 911 for immediate assistance.

Online Resources and Apps

Toronto offers a variety of online resources and mobile apps to enhance the visitor experience. Here are some useful platforms for travel information, navigation, and exploration:

1. Tourism Toronto Website:
- The official Tourism Toronto website (https://www.seetorontonow.com/) provides comprehensive information on attractions, events, accommodations, and travel tips.

2. Google Maps:
- Google Maps is a versatile navigation app that helps visitors explore the city, find directions, discover nearby attractions, and access real-time traffic information.

3. TTC Official App:
- The Toronto Transit Commission (TTC) has an official app that offers real-time transit information, schedules, and service alerts to help navigate the city's public transportation system.

4. BlogTO:

- BlogTO (https://www.blogto.com/) is an online platform that provides insights into Toronto's latest events, restaurant reviews, nightlife, and local news.

5. NOW Magazine:
- NOW Magazine (https://nowtoronto.com/) offers event listings, reviews, and insights into Toronto's arts, culture, and entertainment scene.

6. Toronto.com:
- Toronto.com (https://www.toronto.com/) is a comprehensive guide offering information on events, dining, attractions, and local happenings in the city.

7. Yelp:
- Yelp (https://www.yelp.ca/toronto) is a user-generated review platform that helps visitors discover and review local businesses, restaurants, and attractions.

8. Transit App:
- The Transit App provides real-time information on public transportation, including bus and subway schedules, service alerts, and trip planning.

9. Uber and Lyft:

- Ride-sharing apps like Uber (https://www.uber.com/ca/en/) and Lyft (https://www.lyft.com/) provide convenient transportation options in and around the city.

10. Toronto Public Library Online Resources:

- The Toronto Public Library website (https://www.torontopubliclibrary.ca/) offers a range of online resources, including e-books, audiobooks, and access to digital content.

11. Weather Apps:

- Weather apps such as The Weather Network (https://www.theweathernetwork.com/ca) or AccuWeather (https://www.accuweather.com/) provide up-to-date weather forecasts for planning outdoor activities.

12. Eventbrite:

- Eventbrite (https://www.eventbrite.ca/) allows users to discover and book tickets for events, concerts, and activities happening in Toronto.

13. ParkMobile:

- ParkMobile (https://parkmobile.io/) offers a convenient way to pay for parking in Toronto using a mobile device.

14. Toronto Parking Authority Green P App:
- The Green P app provides information on available parking spaces, rates, and payment options for Toronto Parking Authority lots.

These online resources and apps cater to various aspects of a visitor's journey, from planning and navigation to discovering local events and services in Toronto. Utilizing these tools can contribute to a seamless and enjoyable travel experience.

CONCLUSION

In the heart of Toronto's vibrant streets, where the echoes of diverse cultures harmonize and the skyline stands as a testament to a city that never sleeps, your journey becomes a story, woven with the threads of exploration and discovery. As we bid farewell to this enchanting guide, envision the memories awaiting you in every corner of Toronto.

Toronto, with its iconic skyline adorned by the CN Tower, the cultural tapestry of neighborhoods like Kensington Market and the Distillery District, and the welcoming spirit of its people, beckons you to immerse yourself in its embrace. The allure of its theaters, the rhythm of its music, the flavors of its diverse cuisines — they all intertwine to create a narrative that is uniquely yours.

Venture through the diverse neighborhoods, where history and modernity coexist seamlessly. Feel the pulse of the Entertainment District, savor the artistic ambiance of Yorkville, and wander the charming streets of Leslieville. Each step is an invitation to uncover the city's many facets.

In Toronto, every sunrise whispers promises of new adventures, while each sunset paints the sky with the hues of a day well spent. The CN Tower, standing tall amidst the city's heartbeat, becomes a silent witness to the stories told in every corner.

As your journey in Toronto unfolds, may you find solace in the rhythm of its streets, inspiration in its cultural tapestry, and a sense of belonging in the warmth of its hospitality. Toronto is more than a destination; it's an embrace, a celebration of diversity, and a canvas waiting for your unique imprint.

As you leave Toronto, carry with you not just the souvenirs gathered along the way but the echoes of laughter in Nathan Phillips Square, the taste of multicultural cuisines, and the vibrant colors of its festivals. Toronto, with its open arms and endless possibilities, awaits your return.

May the memories forged in Toronto linger in your heart, and may this guide be the compass guiding you back to the enchanting embrace of a city that captures the essence of both dreams and reality. Until we meet again, Toronto awaits your next chapter, your next adventure. Safe travels, and may your journey be as extraordinary as the city that stole your heart.

Farewell and Safe Travels!

Farewell, dear traveler, as you embark on the next leg of your journey. May the echoes of Toronto's vibrant streets, the taste of its diverse cuisines, and the warmth of its hospitality linger in your heart.

As you carry the memories of the CN Tower reaching for the sky and the cultural richness of neighborhoods like Kensington Market, know that Toronto will forever be a part of your personal narrative.

Safe travels on the roads that lie ahead, and may your adventures be filled with joy, discovery, and the enchantment that only travel can bring. Toronto bids you adieu with open arms, ready to welcome you back whenever your heart yearns for its embrace.

Until we meet again, may your path be adorned with new stories, and may the memories of your time in Toronto be a guiding light on your journey.

Farewell, and may your travels be filled with wonder and delight!

WELCOME TO TORONTO